With the ladder now in the crater, the team was executing the extract drill. Taylor got on the ladder first. Fastening himself with a safety rope and snap link, he was quickly followed by Rush and Reed and Ayers, who checked to ensure the ropes were secured to the ladder. Heavy fire was pouring into the crater from the uphill side, and we returned fire frantically.

Finally, the Cobras screamed in and pulled into a sixty-degree nose-down hover on two sides of the crater and began to saturate the heavy jungle on its edges with minigun fire. Given all the enemy activity, Miller and I understood that the extract was our first and last chance. The heavy thud of the Cobras' 2.75-inch rockets was followed by the whine of shrapnel, which cut vicious swaths of foliage, then streaked ruthlessly through the air around the crater.

Despite the suppressive fire, the extract choppers and gunships were now taking steady hits from ground fire. Ayers snapped himself onto the ladder, then fired several bursts at the muzzle flashes around the crater. Miller looked at me and yelled above the din of battle, "Let's get the hell outta here!"

FIRST FORCE RECON COMPANY

Sunrise at Midnight

Dr. Bill Peters

IVY BOOKS • NEW YORK

An Ivy Book
Published by The Ballantine Publishing Group
Copyright © 1999 by Dr. Bill Peters
Foreword copyright © 1999 by Lt. Gen. Ormond R. Simpson

www.randomhouse.com/BB/

Library of Congress Catalog Card Number: 98-93276

ISBN 0-8041-1873-6

Printed in Canada

First Edition: February 1999

10   9   8   7   6   5   4

Dedicated to
Sgt. Eugene "Mother" Ayers
MIA March 19, 1970

Greater love hath no man than this,
that a man lay down his life for his friends.
John 15:13

In memory of my father, William Joseph Peters, Sr.,
whose final words to me set the course for my life.

To the memory of C. Randy Champe,
whose uncommon valor in Vietnam,
and with the Los Angeles Police Department
on June 13, 1991,
was above and beyond the call of duty.

To the memory of 1st Lt. Leland Thane Wallace.

Contents

	Acknowledgments	ix
	Foreword, by Lt. Gen. Ormond R. Simpson	xi
1	SAN FRANCISCO STATE	1
2	SAYING GOOD-BYE	19
3	WELCOME TO VIETNAM	33
4	SNAPPING IN	55
5	INTO THE QUE SONS	77
6	THE COVENANT	103
7	RECON ROCK AND ROLL	118
8	THE QUE SON FANDANGO	140
9	THE FOURTH OF JULY	167
10	THE PRISONER GRAB	190
11	INTO THE MOUTH OF THE LION	210
12	BITTERSWEET VICTORY	227
	Epilogue	234

Acknowledgments

Before I render thanks to all the others who have helped me, I want to extend my deepest love and appreciation to my wife, Barbara, and to our sons, Tony and Paul, for their constant encouragement and inspiration during the many years that it took to develop this account of the brave men of 1st Force Recon Company.

To my mother, Lucille, and sister, Jan, whose unconditional love and prayers brought me home; to my in-laws, Joe and Mollie Gonzales, for believing in me and praying for this book; to Maj. Gen. Terrence and Catherine Murray for their love and support; to my partners: Harry and JoEllen Valentine, Bill and Peggy Hoover, Sue Champe, and Col. Joe Smith; to Ed Batal, the class of 1968's official point man; to Loretta and Martin Tencza, for their many prayers and support; to Owen Lock, for believing in this book.

Foreword

During my tenure as commanding general, 1st Marine Division in Vietnam, I was privileged to know many brave men. Quite naturally, most of these were to be seen in the units most frequently in direct contact with the enemy—infantry and recon. This is not to say that they were not present in other units, for I am certain they were. It was simply that they were not often put in position to demonstrate their personal courage.

However, I thought then—and think now—that there seemed to be an unusual concentration of such men in 1st Force Recon. This relatively small, tightly knit, and highly motivated group seemed somehow to be a breed a bit apart. These people were in superb physical condition; their skills were honed to a fine edge. They were always ready—even eager—to undertake the most dangerous and difficult missions. I never saw higher morale anywhere in the area. The efforts of 1st Force Recon brought us information not available from any other source. This contributed directly to many successful operations and, I am convinced, saved lives of fellow Marines.

I recall one deep-penetration patrol with the code name Sunrise. After several days on site, the patrol had essentially accomplished its mission and was moving slowly toward the predetermined pickup point. In this process, it was detected and attacked by a much larger NVA force. Thus began some of the most tense hours in my memory. Sunrise was hit about 1730 hours. The word reached me about 1800 plus, while I was at dinner. I went immediately to the operations center in the huge bunker, which was the heart of the 1st Marine Division command post. My position was a high captain's chair where I could scan the huge operations map and also hear all the radio transmissions. It was immediately clear that, at least for the time being, the only way we could help Sunrise was with air support. The patrol was on the far side of effective artillery fire. In the heavily wooded area, relief by a helicopter-transported ground element was out of the question before first light. I doubted that Sunrise could hold out that long. We turned to the 1st Wing, which responded in outstanding fashion. Helicopter gunships made radio contact with, and got a reasonable fix on, the team's position. By this time, the command posts of III MAF, 1st Wing, and 1st MarDiv were all alerted and monitoring all possible radio traffic. In our case, there was no panic, but in the op center the air was heavy with concern. The patrol leader reported that he had two KIA, five WIA, including himself as we learned later, and three able-bodied. He was moving by small increments in the direction of the pickup point, but it was apparent that he was not going to be able to reach it before he was overwhelmed.

The leader was seeking some spot where an emergency pickup might be possible. Gunships were relieved on station as ordnance and fuel ran low. A-4s dropped fragmentation bombs as we attempted to put a ring of fire around the beleaguered patrol. (My word—not theirs.) Two CH-46 transport helicopters were on station and orbiting, hoping for the chance to make an emergency extraction.

A faithful sergeant stood by my chair all night, bringing

me countless cups of coffee. As the hours wore on, it was clear that we had to at least attempt a pickup. Time was running out for Sunrise. The patrol leader picked a spot from which he thought he *might* be able to get his people aboard a hovering CH-46. The weather was marginal at best as the spot was on a steep mountainside where the chopper could not possibly land. Then, in an incredible feat of airmanship, the pilot of one CH-46 dropped his rear ramp and actually backed into the side of the mountain. The crewmen, watching from the rear of the aircraft, reported to the pilot that there was no clearance between the rear rotor blades and the trees. The pilot held the bird out of ground effect as Sunrise struggled aboard while four gunships flew a tight firing circle. The bodies of the KIA were brought aboard first, then the WIAs (except the team leader). Last to board was the team leader, backing up the ramp and firing all the while. Two members of the aircraft crew had crossed the ramp to help with the KIAs and WIAs. At last, all were aboard the aircraft. The pilot let the aircraft fall off into the valley as he closed the rear ramp. Then he pulled up and started home, closely escorted by the four gunships as the flight leader sent the welcome message: "Sunrise—homeward bound!" A shout of joy and relief swept the op center.

I left my chair for the first time and moved to a small balcony that gave a clear view of Da Nang below and of the 1st Medical Battalion and its lighted helo pad. After a few moments, we saw the lights and heard the sound of the five helicopters at the far end of the mountain. The CH-46 headed direct for the lighted pad, where corpsmen and doctors were waiting. The four gunships escorted the CH-46 almost to the deck and then pulled up and away in a final triumphant salute to success and teamwork!

I knew the tears were streaming down my face, but I

was smiling. My faithful sergeant was there in the darkness. He put his hand lightly on my shoulder and said quietly, "Sir, thank God we got to see Sunrise at midnight." It was 2400.

I went to the hospital and talked to the team leader, who thought it a routine patrol until the end and apologized for all the "trouble"! Such was the fiber of 1st Force Recon!

Obviously I have high regard for the officers and men of 1st Force Recon. They were splendid Marines—a credit to themselves, their outfit, their Corps, and their country. I am proud to have been able to serve with them.

Ormond R. Simpson
Lt. General, USMC (Ret)
May 8, 1987

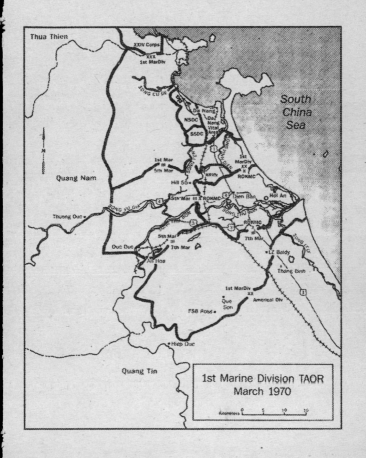

Thua Thien

XXIV Corps
XXX
1st MarDiv

SONG CU DE

Da Nang
Da Nang Vital Area
NSDC
SSDC

South China Sea

1st Mar
III
5th Mar

SONG YEN

1st MarDiv
XX
X
ROKMC

ARVN

Hill 55

Quang Nam

5th Mar III X ROKMC

Dien Ban

Hoi An

Thuong Duc

SONG VU GIA

TUY LOAN

7th Mar III

SONG THU BON

ROKMC III 7th Mar

Duc Duc

5th Mar III 7th Mar

LZ Baldy

Thang Binh

An Hoa

1st MarDiv
XX
American Div

Que Son

FSB Ross

1

Hiep Duc

Quang Tin

**1st Marine Division TAOR
March 1970**

Kilometers 0   5   10   15

CHAPTER 1

San Francisco State

The Vietnam War started for me long before I attended the Marine Corps Officers Candidate School at Quantico, Virginia, in the summer of 1967. Months before I reported for active duty in June 1968, I had more than experienced the sting of battle over that very unpopular war. From the spring of 1966 through the spring of 1968, a second front for the war in Vietnam was fought on the college campuses across the United States. I attended and graduated from San Francisco State, one of the most progressive colleges in the country at that time. That is where Vietnam began for me.

On March 22, 1968, a light breeze rushed across the wide lawn in front of the San Francisco State Commons and chilled the damp March midafternoon air. Beside the walk, seventy-five feet from the near continuous traffic through the Commons entrance, two U.S. Marine recruiters were passing out promotional information and answering occasional questions posed by students interested in Marine officer programs. Captains Dick Hogens and Gary Lawson, officer selection officers for the Marine Corps San Francisco Recruiting Service, had a standing beer bet, whenever they went "body snatching" on State's notoriously radical campus, concerning how long it would

1

take for the usual confrontations instigated by Students for a Democratic Society (SDS) to occur. I had positioned myself just inside the Commons, a few feet from Hogens and Lawson, ready to come to their assistance if the protesters got out of hand. The seasoned Marines acknowledged my presence through the glass doors without calling any attention to me.

Hogens, a picture-book, six-foot, 190-pound, jut-jawed infantryman with a high-and-tight haircut and little tolerance for campus radicals, normally bet short-term and won. After a thirteen-month Vietnam tour as a rifle company commander from '66 to '67, when the war had heated up, he did not suffer lightly the usual liberal idealistic moralizing about the justness of the war. He was a Marine, he proudly told his assailants: he went to the war, took care of his men, killed when he had to, and came home reassigned to recruiting duty. His focus in Vietnam, he would say, was always his men and doing his job. He was committed to his profession and to his country. Many times he felt more under fire in the frantic antiwar atmosphere of San Francisco then he recalled feeling in combat.

Captain Gary Lawson, a class of '64 Naval Academy graduate and Huey gunship pilot, also a Vietnam combat vet, in spite of military roots deeply formed during his Annapolis years, was more philosophical about students' rights to dissent. "Hoge," he'd frequently say, "these are just idealistic young college kids trying to find themselves. Give them time and a little more experience and they'll come around."

Hogens saw it differently. In his view, at least several of the SDS leadership, including Jake McKenney, a chief antiwar, antidraft, antimilitary strategist, were professional students. McKenney was in his late twenties or early thirties, and in the SDS during the chaotic sixties, he had finally found himself a niche with genuine stature. Hogens went nose to nose with McKenney, a philosophy major, several times before being convinced that McKenney planned to make a college career of igniting anarchic fires in the bellies of every naive nineteen-year-old State student in search of a cause. Stealing what he considered a particularly chic term from the Soviet Communist lexicon, McKenney reveled in staging agitprop events to ridicule and undermine his targets. Military recruiters, like Hogens and Lawson, and representatives of agencies and industries associated with supporting the Vietnam War were inevitably besieged by McKenney and his SDS antiwar, antiestablishment activists on campus. Hogens and Lawson wondered when their SDS assailants and their sometimes not-fully-committed followers found time for school.

Hogens found it unthinkable that State's students would act so radically toward the school's, and the government's, authority: they were making such a sham of their college educations and they seemed never to be in class. Lawson, who'd spent his "college years" at Annapolis, taking nineteen to twenty-one hours a semester and enduring all the usual indignities and deprivations that entailed, found student antics entertaining if a bit misguided and irresponsible. To its credit, the SDS did not confine its dissent to the Vietnam War: *anything* establishment-based was fair game. A week earlier, the Dow Chemical headhunter had been run off campus, in spite of the school administration's sanctioning his visit. The San Francisco State administration articulated its policies—such as keeping the campus open to recruiters of all kinds—adequately, but it consistently shirked its duty to enforce them, particularly in succumbing to the overbearing pressures of the radical left.

The SDS was taking on a variety of causes under McKenney and his subordinate leaders to bring "equality" to the campus and to give the students a voice in what he commonly referred to as "all spheres of the San Francisco State educational process." As leader of the San Francisco chapter of the Students for a Democratic Society, McKenney took very seriously his role in what the SDS referred to as "preaching and practicing the policies of disruption." The causes he and his deputies had targeted reached into all vital areas of student and campus activity. The real student issue at State, as it was nationwide throughout the college and university systems, was control, and who was—and should have the right—to call the shots, the traditional agencies within the school administration or the students.

As Hogens watched a wave of about 150 SDS-led students flowing toward him and Larson, he suspected that business was soon going to get brisk. "Hey, Gary," Hogens said, "take a look down the Commons. You can buy me my first pint of Guinness at O'Toole's today."

"Wait a minute, Hoge. Who says I'm buying? If we go another thirty minutes, you buy, Grunt!"

Lawson watched the small sea of students move steadily toward them. He really didn't expect to win the day's bet, but he wasn't ready to roll over to Hogens yet. "My guess, Hoge, is that it's just coincidence we're alone on this beautiful lawn in front of the State Commons and the SDSers are in the area politicking again. This speech-making stuff is the daily bill o' fare around here, bro. As I read today's campus rag, the SDSers got bigger fish to fry than two lowly Marine recruiters out to catch a couple of young guys who want to serve their country."

As the SDSers began to close on the recruiters, who stood behind a portable cafeteria table adorned with Marine Corps promotional material, my football teammate, Harry Gualco, Steve Diaz, the former Associated Students treasurer, and I emerged from the front entrance of the Commons. I could see that an SDS confrontation was imminent with the Marines. Hogen and Lawson had signed up Gualco and me a year before. As Gualco and I trotted over to the recruiters, Diaz said he was going to alert the campus police in case things got out of control.

The SDS demonstrators had quickly transited two hundred yards of Commons lawn and closed with the Marine recruiters, enveloping them in a crescent-shaped crowd. Captain Hogens and Captain Lawson stood coolly, prepared for the first volleys as the SDS demonstrators strengthened their verbal assault. Gualco and I took our posts on the flanks of the recruiters.

As an elected member of the student government (Associated Students treasurer), I officially cautioned McKenney not to interrupt an authorized visit by the Marine recruiters. McKenney ignored my appeal; he was intent on driving the recruiters off, just as he had the Dow Chemical representative. McKenney sensed the growing frenzy of his formation of followers. McKenney knew their cause was right—the war was misguided, unjust. He and the officially unrepresented masses had earned their place. They were obligated to change what the establishment would not. Today, McKenney probably thought, we'll win another firefight in the relentless guerrilla war he and his kind had undertaken for the good of all society. Hogens and Lawson, who'd been repeatedly counseled by the senior Marine recruiter to maintain their composure, even when antagonized on campus, kept their cool.

Gualco and I, plus a few friends from the football team, were losing ours.

Once again, I could see that the student sheep were being led by the SDS leadership, McKenney, Tewes, and Stein. That afternoon, McKenney was in the vanguard, demanding that Lawson and Hogens get off the Commons grounds. I was, by then, standing beside Hogens, and intervened. "You know I represent the student government. All of us also know that the military recruiters are permitted to come on campus. They're entitled to conduct business just as are spokesmen the SDS sponsors." I directed my comments at McKenney and Tewes, since they were orchestrating the day's protest. "Why don't all of you get back to class where you belong?"

But the SDS leaders were not to be turned away that easily, then or in the near future. They believed their continuous agitation was having an effect, and the evidence that they might be right was college president Summerskill and the school administration's vacillation and indecisiveness in confronting the SDS as it disrupted officially sanctioned campus activity with increasing frequency. Just the night before, McKenney and Tewes had exhorted their disciples in the auditorium that the SDS was winning and that the time to increase the pressure had come.

McKenney and SDS cochairman Mark Tewes led the chant: "Ho, ho, Ho Chi Minh, the NLF is gonna win. Hey, hey, LBJ, how many kids did you kill today!" Others on the flanks shouted, "Stop killing babies," and "Get out of Vietnam."

As the company of protesters began its march down the parade grounds, from fifteen feet deep in the crowd a young pimply-faced coed with iron-straightened dirty-blond hair and wire-rim granny glasses awkwardly lofted a cellophane bag of flour toward us, striking Captain

Hogens on the left shoulder. It broke open, covering the meticulously uniformed Marine and two supporters in a cloud of powder. Stimulated by the coed's courageous act, a dozen other SDS soldiers pelted the Marines and their friends with flour.

Then a long-haired SDSer with a tie-dyed shirt, apparently inspired by the skirmishing, moved toward me and, when just several feet away, waved the Viet Cong flag in front of my face. At first I assumed the staff of the flag was a broom handle, but I quickly saw that it was three-quarter-inch pipe. While the two Marines articulately fended off the charges that they were war criminals, the unkempt students swarmed around them.

I remained at Hogens's and Lawson's side, but when the SDSer waved the flag past my nose a second time, I stepped forward and planted a pretty good right cross flush on his mouth, launching him backward headlong into the crowd. Bedlam ensued, and an SDSer next to the Viet Cong flag-waver began throwing punches at me wildly. Harry Gualco, who stood on the other side of the Marines, was also pelted with one of the bags of flour, which now rained on them. Seeing me and the recruiters being assaulted, he joined the growing fray, punching someone who had me collared.

Most of the demonstrators began to disperse when the fighting began, but a number engaged me, Gualco, and the few students who came to the recruiters' aid. The melee was only a minute old when the campus police cars raced up to the Commons, sirens blaring. The crowd was quickly driven off with little physical damage to the few serious combatants.

I was ushered into the school president's office by Summerskill's executive assistant. Summerskill sat behind a huge mahogany desk and officiously waved me to sit down across the desk from him. I knew Summerskill was being pressured by campus radicals and was, at least, considering temporary dismissal. The student newspaper announced two days after the protest and altercation that Summerskill had ordered an inquiry and had promised the SDS "appropriate disciplinary action." Of course, the SDS leaders were demanding specific action against me. The SDS was also seeking the dismissal or suspension of a handful of athletes who had allegedly, without provocation, assaulted innocent protesters. The SDS claimed none of their members or followers instigated the fight or threw any punches.

"Mr. Peters," Summerskill began formally, wanting to put me on the defensive. "This won't be a long meeting. I wanted you to know officially, however, that I've appointed a committee under the dean of students to investigate your involvement in the fight earlier this week."

I didn't respond, although I thought to myself that it was not surprising Summerskill said the investigation was to focus on me and not the incident in its entirety or the role of the SDS. I looked at Summerskill steadily, expecting next a whitewash of SDS involvement. I was confident, given the scale of the incident and knowing he still enjoyed the support of many on campus—both inside and outside the student government—that Summerskill would find as many in support of his actions as opposed.

"You're probably aware," the president continued, "that the SDS has filed a very serious grievance against you, the student government, and a few other students. If the committee confirms this allegation, I may have to suspend or dismiss you even though your graduation is just a month away."

My stomach began to turn as much at Summerskill's

fawning submission to radical pressures as to the recognition that my degree and, much more important just then, my commissioning as a Marine Corps officer could be delayed. "President Summerskill," I snapped back, "I assume you were also told I tried to mediate, and stop, what was becoming an explosive situation. You really don't believe that the SDS did not at least partly instigate the incident." I was incredulous.

Summerskill ignored my retort, preferring to focus on what the SDS described to him as my uncalled-for assault. "Mr. Peters, physical measures are unacceptable even when you strongly disagree with someone. That's why some off-campus extremists have been arraigned for attacking the school's newspaper staff." I couldn't believe Summerskill was comparing the fight on the Commons lawn with the extremists' brutal assault on Jim Vasco, the editor of *The Golden Gater*, the school rag. The assault was in retaliation for what the extremist leadership said was biased reporting of revolutionary issues. I wasn't going to permit Summerskill to pursue the comparison unchallenged.

"If you'd been at the SDS demonstration, you'd understand that there is no comparison to what Ken Garnette and his henchmen did to the *Gater* editor." They had put the 135-pound journalism major in the hospital. Now I was whipping mad.

Summerskill continued to mouth SDS claims: "Mr. Peters, the SDS has numerous witnesses . . ."

I was aghast at Summerskill's naive belief in the SDS account. "Weren't you told that the SDSers were aggressively trying to intimidate and embarrass the Marine recruiters?" I asked. Summerskill stared at me, unconvinced, as I pressed my argument. "They crowded around them, and when they became frustrated with the debate, they threw bags of flour at them and wiped out their uniforms."

My voice trembled with anger as I recalled the clash. "One of them even spit on Captain Hogens."

"The SDS leaders tell a very different story," Summerskill interjected. I didn't acknowledge the president's point. "I've never been to war," I said, "but I am a Marine. It was bad enough to see students taunting the recruiters, but when an SDSer waved a six-foot pipe with a Viet Cong flag attached to it within inches of my face, I lost it. Yeah, I hit him in the mouth, and I'd do it again if I had the chance."

Summerskill, who probably could not recall having had a fistfight in his life, certainly not as an adult college student and student legislator, remained unpersuaded by my rationale. "Bill, you and your jock—" Summerskill caught and corrected himself, then continued. "—athlete cohorts victimized peaceful protesters who were fully within their rights to demonstrate on campus. I'm told by the SDS cochairmen, Jake McKenney and Mark Tewes, that your attack was savage and entirely unprovoked. Even after your assault, the SDS attempted to stop the fight, not continue it."

I unfolded the copy of the *The Gater*, which I had tucked in the book I carried, stood up, and placed the paper on Summerskill's desk. The front-page photograph of the SDS-Marine confrontation clearly showed an SDS student cocking his fist to hit me. I had circled my assailant and myself in red ink so Summerskill couldn't miss them. I also wrote the SDS student's name on the photo.

"President Summerskill, if the administration had done what you'd agreed to with the Associated Students and set the Marines up in the athletic administration area, you would not have had a problem. Instead you parked them on the Commons lawn, which is the SDS battlefield here at State."

Summerskill responded, "I personally see no reason why we should make special accommodations for military recruiters."

"Then these campus clashes will persist, I promise you." Summerskill then launched into a well-rehearsed pitch on my special responsibilities as an official in student government. I realized Summerskill hadn't seriously listened to a word of my explanation.

I was done defending myself. I knew I'd made a mistake hitting the SDSer who'd taunted me and the Marine recruiters with the Viet Cong flag. I couldn't change that. I was confident the committee, if unbiased, would conclude both factions were partly at fault for the nasty incident.

Before I left Summerskill's office, I decided to make a couple points in closing. I told the president the investigative committee, if it was balanced, would find the Marine officers did nothing more than defend themselves. In fact, although they'd wrestled free of the crowd, neither officer had even thrown a punch in self-defense. Summerskill's contemplated plan to prohibit Marine recruiters for an indefinite period of time from doing business on campus was without basis. Besides, I reminded Summerskill, the great majority of students and faculty welcomed the Marines and other military recruiters.

I also urged the president to protect military- and defense-related recruiters, using campus police if necessary, as the State College System chancellor and Governor Reagan had instructed. Given his political and philosophical instincts, Summerskill had strenuously rejected that option to date. Having frequently heard Summerskill's impassioned defense of the rights of campus dissidents, particularly in opposing the war, I told the president I understood his commitment to the rights of free speech and assembly. I asked Summerskill to take whatever actions were necessary to protect those rights for all on campus from those like SDS who would deny them. I then rose and walked out of the president's office.

As I descended the steps of the administration building under a gray San Francisco sky, I felt weary for the first time in my three years at State. The enthusiasm with which I had begun my senior year, heightened by my role in student government, had died. The San Francisco State campus, I concluded, mirrored the national landscape: through their persistent intimidation tactics, the relatively small but extremely vocal and aggressive radical minorities at State, like the radicals nationwide, were getting far more clout than they deserved. Aided by an extreme faction of the faculty at San Francisco State, their influence was disproportionate—and to the detriment of the student body at large. And for the first time, I was beginning to feel that in the near future my efforts as a student government representative would have little influence on changing that.

The campus continued to boil with unrest. The altercation between myself and the SDS had only served to fuel the existing unrest that the sixties generation was facing. I moved quickly from the college administration building to my office located in an isolated old Quonset hut behind the Commons. Pam, my college sweetheart, was sitting at my desk, patiently waiting for me to return from Summerskill's meeting. She jumped up to greet me. When I hugged her, I could feel that she was trembling. "What's wrong?" I asked.

Tearfully she replied, "Some guys were here looking for you. Bill, you have got to get out of here now. I think they were armed."

I tried to comfort her by saying, "Nobody is going to get to me. Come on, let's go get a hamburger and call it a day."

But she said, "I saw a pistol handle sticking out of the waistband of one of those guys, Bill. He didn't look like a student. We have to get out of here. This thing is getting out of hand."

"Okay, I believe you, let's go," I replied, as I motioned to a side door out of the office.

Before we could escape, the front door of my office flew open, and about a dozen angry-looking men crowded into the room. I gave Pam a quick shove out the side door and stepped quickly behind my desk. Although I had put a few feet between myself and my uninvited guests, I was still trapped behind my desk. Pam ran toward the Commons cafeteria, anxiously looking for someone who could help. My eyes searched for a familiar face in the sea of faces filling the office. Finally a skinny, longhaired, pimple-faced kid wearing a green military field jacket and black beret stepped forward. He placed his hands on my desk and leaned forward, putting himself within striking distance of me. I recognized him and said, "Okay, Garnette. If you think what you did to Jim Vasco up at *The Gater* newspaper office is going to work here, think again." Garnette was the leader of a loose coalition of campus extremists and community-based crackpots that was being questioned about the merciless beating of *The Gater* editor. Garnette fired back at me, "Shut up and listen, fool. You're outnumbered, and we are in control. It's not going to go well for you. Before we get to that, we want you to know why." I looked past his seething face for help. Suddenly a tall dark figure filled the doorway. It was William Dodson, a six-foot-six-inch-tall, 295-pound defensive tackle whom I had played shoulder to shoulder with for the past two football seasons. A white, toothy grin was painted on his black face. Behind Dodson, I could pick out more of my football teammates. Dodson began to push his way through the crowd toward me. Six other beefy players followed him.

I smiled at Garnette and said, "Mr. Garnette, you were about to tell me why you and your buddies were going to mess me up. Would you like to continue that conversation?" Garnette glared at me and then turned and pushed his way toward the side door of my office. I reached for the knob, holding the door closed. Now he and I were nose to nose, and I said with real conviction, "You lose, fool." Then I turned the knob on the door and shoved it open. There stood Pam. Garnette brushed by her as he exited. Pam shook and stuttered as she said, "I—I—got William Dodson to come and help you, I—I—was really scared. A-A-Are you okay?" The rest of Garnette's thugs quickly fled my office. Pam had been right about one other thing; I had spotted the pistol in the waistband of one of Garnette's flunkies. That afternoon, I really began fearing for Pam. That was the last time I ever endangered her over campus politics. The events of that day spelled the end of my fighting the Vietnam War on the campus of San Francisco State.

I walked Pam to her car that day, and neither one of us said a word. Somehow we both knew that things would never be the same for us. I think we both knew that the war in Vietnam was going to become up front and personal for me real soon. We kissed and said good-bye the way we had hundreds of times over the past three years in that student parking lot, but our carefree college days ended that day.

I drove out of San Francisco State's main gate and began to focus on my military calling, as the SDS was completing the formation of its on-campus antidraft union, designed to combat Selective Service. While SDS cochairman Max Stein addressed a gathering of 160 male seniors and grad students, the young SDS cadre were passing out literature on how to beat the draft: the options included the Canadian exile route, legal mechanisms, jail protests, and the underground organization said to be growing within the active military itself. Stein concluded by announcing that alternatives were really multiplying. "France," Stein said, "would even offer political asylum and work permits. The future is bright for the strong who choose to resist." When I learned of the meeting, I felt that he failed to recognize—certainly to acknowledge—that several generations of Americans had died in military service so that he would have the privilege to hold such a meeting.

It was a confusing, crazy time for some, but I was confident in my chosen direction. I turned onto Highway 50, threw the stickshift into fourth gear, and headed for home. Looking back at the tumultuous events of my last semester and its near continuous confrontations with campus extremists had not shaken my faith in the future.

However, I still could not reconcile the actions or the mentality of the dissident leadership. What troubled me most was the unquestioning, self-righteous view that the SDS cadre, especially McKenney and Tewes, took of America's involvement in the war. I was not indifferent toward my contemporaries' right to dissent, but I found their methods unacceptable and their intellectual arrogance frightening. To them, America's "wrongness" in being there and the North Vietnamese's rightness were entirely unambiguous.

I was stunned by the SDS leadership's intolerance of other views. To me, the issues were more complex. While my instincts propelled me to support the administration's position and, therefore, my country's, I also grappled with the many uncertainties. My father's admonition while I was growing up that there simply were few absolutes in the world seemed applicable to issues surrounding the war. I knew, however, that I would follow both my heart and intellect: I would go to Vietnam and serve my country in what I perceived as its time of need. I would also go in search of myself as other young men of other times had done before me.

I knew that my differences with Garnette and his brand of politics were not personal, but they were unbridgeable. Garnette was convinced that I, like my student government contemporaries, was biased and instinctively opposed to all of his initiatives. Because of my own olive skin and Portuguese descent, I had been viciously called "a black s.o.b." by the Irish community in my hometown most of my life, so I had little tolerance for accusations that hinted I was racially biased; the accusation was simply a tactic used to project guilt on me that I was unwilling to accept. The extremists, through Garnette, had continuously challenged my student government voting record as it related to their revolutionary programs. I was tired of defending myself and having to point out my high standing among many of the minority students on campus, particularly those who had become my close friends through the school's football program.

I recognized that Garnette and I could never find common ground professionally or personally. Garnette was not a California country boy like myself. Garnette came to San Francisco State embittered over his childhood. He had an ax to grind and probably chose State because it lined up with the escalating social and political movements of the 1960s. Garnette thrived in State's hothouse political climate. I finally wanted relief from it. The recent threats on my life and the safety of those I loved had worn thin my tolerance. On the other hand, I had to admit that it felt good to crush that guy's face. Perhaps it would be a while before he again waved a Viet Cong flag in front of someone's nose. In any case, I knew I was ready to strike back at those things that I perceived as threats to my future or to that of my family. I knew that San Francisco State was not the proper arena in which to wrestle with my enemies. There was a battlefield designed for me where I would have my convictions and integrity thoroughly tested. It was called Vietnam, and I knew my destiny was intertwined with that distant war.

I turned east toward the peacefulness of my home in the Livermore Valley, about forty miles from San Francisco. I recalled my father's wise counsel: sometimes even a strong man's best choice is to walk away from a dilemma that offers no apparent solution. "Live to fight another day, kid," he always said. Maybe my dad was right. There comes a time when it's better for a man to cut his losses in one area to concentrate on another where he might make a difference. My dad said he held no naive belief that I could affect the outcome of the war. He did concede that I would have a direct effect on the Marines that I would lead in combat. He encouraged me not to ever ask the men under my command to do something I was unwilling to do myself. I took his advice on that subject very seriously. Recalling my father's words gave me confidence again.

I knew that neither I nor my philosophical partners at State had the last answer on all the issues surrounding Vietnam. I did believe that my position lacked the absolute arrogance of the SDS and the emotional intransigence of my country's political extremists. I was no longer willing to be surrounded by San Francisco State's hypocritical faculty and dissident students. There were some on the faculty who fueled members of my generation with thoughts that proved to be insane. They lived an affluent, tenured lifestyle in the expensive Park Merced apartments overlooking the campus, while their disciples on campus paid a heavy price to live out their teachers' social agenda. In the late spring of 1968, my father sensed my struggles at State and said, "Bill, it's time to fold your tent." It was hard for me to walk away from the standoff on campus. In my gut, that didn't feel good, but in my heart, I knew he was right.

As my car flew over a sudden rise on the coast road, in my rearview mirror I saw the San Francisco skyline, tall buildings that seemed to reach for the open sea to the west. I took a deep breath, then, confident of my course, continued heading east.

CHAPTER 2

Saying Good-bye

I lay quietly, listening to the sounds of summer as birds chirped and brushed their wings against the lush arbor sheltering my bedroom window from the early-morning sun. The familiar sound of the radio station KYA broadcasting out of San Francisco could be heard playing the sixties favorite "Eve of Destruction" by Barry McGuire. The song ended and the 7:00 A.M. news cut through the cool summer morning air like a blazing arrow when the announcer reported, "Bobby Kennedy is dead."

The words shocked me into full consciousness. The next thing I knew, I was standing in the kitchen, staring at the radio. "It's true, Bobby Kennedy was shot last night in Los Angeles while campaigning for the Democratic nomination for president," my mother said. Mom stood in her pantry, wiping the tears from her eyes. She was a tall, beautiful, olive-skinned woman in her late forties. Her soft brown eyes seemed to be pleading with me as she said, "Bobby Kennedy might have pulled us out of Vietnam, son. People don't care anymore. Don't try to be a hero, Bill. This damn war doesn't look good. Bobby Kennedy is gone, but I'm worried about you."

"What in the hell is going on in this country? Wasn't JFK enough? In March, it was Martin Luther King. What is going on? I can't believe this extremist bull crap. No

19

one tolerates anybody's views anymore." Mom tried to calm me, but to no avail. Emotions generated by the several years of intolerance and violence that I had witnessed at San Francisco State were boiling to the surface.

Only one person could talk sense to me when I got like that, my lifelong buddy Lee Wallace, who lived up the street. We were inseparable. We partied and played football together in high school and college. We had shared summer jobs and lifted weights together for years, living our dream of playing for the Far Western championship football team at San Francisco State. But that particular morning, I would not expect to hear Lee's '57 Ford come roaring down the street; Lee had traded the old Ford for a multimillion-dollar Phantom Jet and a pair of gold Marine Corps aviator wings. Every football season for the past eight years, we had played together. The hometown newspaper always carried a story during football season about Lee and me. We had survived years of battle not only on the gridiron but also on the streets of our hometown. Livermore was a cowboy town and the home of a huge annual rodeo. Lee was a cowboy at heart. He wore boots and a cowboy hat to class at San Francisco State. We were legendary for fistfights and football. We were always living on the edge.

In the summer of 1967, after our college football eligibility expired, we joined the Marine Corps and completed Officers Candidate School at Quantico, Virginia. Whatever we did, we did it together. Lee preceded me to active-duty status by six months, which allowed him to get his flight training. I would follow with the much shorter infantry course six months later. We figured we would both arrive in Vietnam the summer of 1969. Lee, the jet jockey, would be running air strikes while I would be finding the targets as a ground officer. Somehow destiny had kept us together all those years, and our youthful zeal would carry us through the war. We thought we were bulletproof. Apparently, Bobby Kennedy was not, and the day after his death was a lonely day for me; Lee Wallace was three thousand miles away fulfilling his destiny as a Marine Corps fighter pilot.

Not wanting to further upset my mother, I decided to go for a run. I quickly slipped into my jogging gear, burst out of the kitchen door, and headed south on North Livermore Avenue. The run was no fun that day. I ran along a lonely stretch of familiar road winding its way through the vineyards and farmland of the Livermore Valley. My mind was racing much faster than my legs. After the first mile, my thoughts switched from Kennedy to a much more parochial interest. How do I fit Pam into my life? I care about her, but I don't have room for her right now. I'll be in Vietnam in six months. I've got to focus, and she's so needy. Everything was changing. I concluded that I had to make some choices. As my legs moved faster, I hoped that I could somehow outrun the uncertainty that flooded my thoughts. Pam had been there for me during my three tumultuous years at San Francisco State, even when it was life threatening during the riots. She hung out with me during the worst and the best of times. I started thinking about the best of times. I had been instrumental in boosting her self-confidence to run for cheerleader at State.* I rationalized our relationship until I decided that she could wait for me to get back from Nam, and then we could talk about marriage. Suddenly I realized my leisurely jog had turned into a sprint. Lost in my thoughts,

---

*That led her eventually to become a cheerleader with the Oakland Raiders professional football team. From there, she landed a job in San Francisco's Playboy Club.

I had run a mile beyond the three-mile landmark. I was stuck running eight miserable miles that morning, and my body ached. Down deep, I knew Pam didn't owe me anything. The war was my thing. I didn't think she was willing to roll the dice for eighteen months, wondering if I'd return in uniform or in a coffin. By the time I reached home, I was unable to escape the reality that soon there would be some major changes in my life.

The Fillmore Auditorium, not far from the San Francisco Haight-Ashbury district, reverberated with the music of the Jefferson Airplane. Grace Slick, the Plane's lead singer, was barely visible in the smoky haze that filled the ancient music mecca. She began to moan her way through her hit song "White Rabbit." Hippies and straight kids filled the dance floor, creating an incredible atmosphere that knew no race, color, or creed. The music of the sixties somehow bridged the gap for a generation that was being torn apart by the war in Vietnam. Locked in mortal combat, Pam and I stood in the midst of the cultural bedlam. Pam pivoted and pushed her way through the crowd. Our words only became audible once we broke into the fresh air out on the street. She pounded her fists against my chest, shouting tearfully, "You aren't asking me to marry you; you aren't taking me with you to Quantico; do I mean anything to you? You love yourself, your Marine Corps. I can't believe anything you tell me anymore. I can't stand this anymore." Pam turned from me and began to walk away. I reached for her and pulled her back to me. I was speechless, and all I could do was hold her in my arms. Most of what she had said was true. Kids began to pour out of the auditorium. Within seconds, the street was full of young people, all enjoying the fresh air and freedom associated with San Francisco in the late 1960s. It was all in sharp contrast to the serious mood surrounding a speechless Marine and his once trusting girlfriend.

San Francisco had never seemed so dank and dreary as it did that night after I dropped Pam off at her apartment in the Sunset district. It seemed like the fog came out of nowhere and hugged the ground a few feet in front of my car. The lights of the city seemed dim as my car climbed the on ramp to the Bay Bridge. What is happening? I thought. I had not spoken a word after Pam's blowup in front of the Fillmore. Somehow, I was going to have to admit that I had probably destroyed my relationship with her. Truthfully, I had made the decision months before to put her on the back burner, but I hadn't been brave enough to tell her. My lack of honor filled every inch of my being. "There is no excuse, no excuse," I murmured as I headed west on Highway 50 toward the Livermore Valley.

Demoralized, I pulled into Livermore a little after midnight, wishing that I had already reported for active duty. My commissioning ceremony, a couple of weeks earlier at the Marine Memorial Club, had sealed my commitment to the Corps for at least three years. But the August report date had been a surprise; I'd thought July would be the latest report date I would receive for duty at the Marine Corps Officers Basic School at Quantico. One thing I had learned last summer at Officers Candidate School was the military principle of hurry up and wait. The control I'd once had over my life was rapidly slipping away.

The unfamiliar feeling that I had in my gut really began to bother me. I began to drive around the back streets of town, reflecting on my last few months of college. The decisions I had made were life-changing. Vietnam, I conceded, was part of my destiny. Because it was my destiny, no one would be able to understand what was drawing me into a war ten thousand miles from home. Not my mom, dad, aunts, uncles, Pam, or my friends; none of them could really understand. But there was one person in town who could possibly relate to my torment, Gary Nelson. Gary and I had gotten close in high school and started college together, but he dropped out of school early in 1965 and fulfilled a family tradition by joining the Marines.

I sped down the empty streets en route to Nelson's house. Gary's brand-new, light blue 1968 Olds Cutlass was sitting in the driveway, a shiny trophy, the spoils of war for his time spent in Vietnam. Wounded in the spring of 1967, Nelson sported a nasty purple scar between his eyes. The money earned in Vietnam had purchased the car, and the USMC logo on the bumper, in his mind, protected it. As I pulled up to his house, I gunned my engine loudly, our old signal. Nelson was a night owl, and I knew he was probably up watching an old John Wayne war movie. He answered the door, puffing on a Camel and flashing a big toothy smile. "Hey, Pete! Come on in," he bellowed. "No, just grab your shoes. I'm buying at Malleys, come on," I replied.

Nelson insisted on driving, so a lot of the conversation on the way to the all-night diner was centered on his new car. "Yeah, we have come a long way since we used to cruise around town in your '53 Ford convertible," I said. The uneasy feeling began to leave me as my old friend drove along the familiar streets, talking about the good times we had shared. Nelson understood what my late-night visit was all about, but he wasn't going to mention it. Some feelings between young warriors are never spoken, they're just shared through the spirit that joins their souls. We were closer than brothers in many ways. I was at the hospital the night Nelson learned that his father had died in an auto accident. We had fought back-to-back dozens of times and somehow found a way to win. Nelson was to me in street fights what Lee Wallace had been to me on the football field. He was someone I didn't have to impress. We sat until the early-morning hours, sipping Malleys's bitter coffee, talking about the Marine Corps and Vietnam. Nelson was holding class on everything from the way a young officer should handle himself around his men to small-unit tactics. I hung on every word and probably learned more practical leadership in that conversation than I had learned in two months of Officers Candidate School the previous summer.

During the next couple of weeks, I began to realize just how deep my roots really went into the rich soil of the Livermore Valley. The Peters family had been in the valley since the turn of the century. My grandfather had died in a horse-and-buggy accident during the depression, leaving my father with the responsibility of raising three sisters and a brother. My grandmother had been a legend in the valley for her tough, no-nonsense approach to life's problems. When the local Catholic priest took my dad's tennis shoes away because he wore them to serve mass as an altar boy, Grandma Peters brought the priest to his knees with a litany of threats. Grandma got the tennis shoes back and an apology from the stunned clergyman. Every part of town had the Peters family brand on it. Bars, plumbing shops, ranches, homes, and land owned by the clan were modest rewards acquired during the post–World War II prosperity of central California. Trying to say good-bye to the family was a job in itself. I shared with my dad one July afternoon how hard it was to find all the family members at home to say good-bye. Bill Peters, Sr., was a true patriarch. He wasn't rich, but he had power and influence. He loved his family very deeply and secretly took great pride in my success. "Quit running all over the valley to say good-bye; we'll have a party at the house," he said. I knew if Dad threw a party, every family member and friend would be there. My dad was a true leader. He always taught me loyalty toward family and friends. The excitement surrounding the party grew during its two-week preparation. I knew it was going to be an evening to remember.

It was my first summer spent at home in three years. San Francisco State had been an all-consuming experience. But by mid-July, I was back in touch with a reality that had eluded me amid the fireworks of one of the most radical college settings of the sixties. There was a sweetness about the Livermore Valley that I had almost forgotten, and I had to consciously resist the comfortable feelings that were beginning to dull my Marine Corps instincts. These were mental qualities that every leader needed. The 1968 Tet offensive that had hit Vietnam just a few months earlier had become a reminder that there was still a real war being waged. I couldn't let the good life of the valley weaken my resolve to lead men in combat. I would repeat to myself, "Fight it, don't give in, stay sharp." The valley had a way of lulling you into a false sense of security, and I knew I couldn't afford that.

In late July, just about the time that I had started to let down my guard, something happened that jerked me back into reality. At 2:00 A.M. one Saturday morning, Gary Nelson and I parked his gleaming Cutlass in front of Malleys. As we exited the vehicle, we were approached by two teenage valley boys. After mumbling a few unintelligible words, one of the teenagers unloaded on Nelson. The Sunday punch appeared to have opened up his war wound. Blood gushed from between his eyes. We shared a second of disbelief, smiled, and nodded at each other as our street-fighter instincts kicked in. These valley boys were too young to recognize the legends they had assaulted. After all, we held the title for street fights in the valley. Where were these kids then? In junior high? In diapers? Nelson, with split-second speed, swept the young punk off his feet, punching him into submission beneath the bumper of the Cutlass. With equal speed, I polished the passenger-side rear fender of the car with the face of the assailant's sidekick. The entire episode was over in less than a minute. Nelson was furious that the punch might have destroyed the skin graft that covered his wound, but I gave the wound a quick examination and assured Nelson that the skin graft was still intact. Relief evident in his voice, Nelson said, "Let's get out of here before the cops show up." Then, like two old veterans, we sped away, leaving the bewildered valley boys in a heap on the ground.

In the days that followed, I roamed around the valley in an effort to get back in touch with my roots. I spent a lot of time with my dad. One evening, we drove into the Black Hills, about ten miles north of the city limits. The familiar shimmy in the front wheels of our World War II–vintage jeep made the drive more than exciting. Dad had to handle the steering wheel like the reins of a bucking bronco. At times, the wheels came precariously close to leaving the narrow paved road. The sheer drop into the deep canyons that cascaded toward the valley floor below made the trip even more dangerous, but Dad always liked to give his boy a little gut check, especially when the jeep roared up the steepest part of the mountain. If I showed any fear, Dad knew that he had won the silent little game. Halfway through one of the extremely sharp turns, the shimmy got so bad that I started to prepare for a crash. Dad, spotting the weakness in me, feigned total loss of control. That was it! I cracked under the pressure. "Look out, Dad!" I shouted as I reached for the wheel. Instantly, he jerked the

jeep back on course. Then came the little gold-tooth smile
that he always flashed when he knew he had won the war
of nerves. You never got a look at that gold incisor unless
he was really pleased about something. Truly the years of
driving that stretch of road in that jeep had helped me
overcome the fear of heights. Something else it had taught
me was that I could trust my father, and I did.

The jeep finally came to a dusty stop on a grassy ridgeline, baked yellow by the scorching August sun. We had
hunted deer in that area of deep, oak-tree-covered gorges
since I was a young boy. I had shot my first deer within a
rock throw of where we were standing. Dad removed from
the gun rack a deer rifle whose battle-scarred stock carried
the evidence of numerous forays into those hills. It was
unspoken, but somehow Dad and I knew this was the last
time we would hunt together. I didn't take my rifle on that
trip; I hadn't wanted to buy deer tags and license for just
one hunt. Once again, and maybe for the last time, I felt
that I could relax and just follow the lead of my father. Dad
led me along the rim of the canyon. At a familiar vantage
point, we stopped to scan the tree line on the other side of
the canyon. I began to recall a cool evening hunt many
years ago where he raised his rifle at that very spot and
took aim at a handsome buck that was raking its antlers
against the low branches of a huge oak several hundred
yards away. From a steady standing position, Dad squeezed
off a single shot, dropping the deer where it stood. I was
just a fifth grader at the time, and I bragged to my friends
for a week about that shot. I was proud of my dad. While
the two of us stood shoulder to shoulder on that grassy hill,
our eyes were fixed on that big old oak, and we silently
shared that glorious moment of days gone by.

Time had passed quickly for me. With just three days
remaining, prior to my scheduled departure for the Marine

Corps Basic School, I decided it was time to say good-bye to Pam. Vietnam hung like a big gray cloud over the lifestyle of the young people in the San Francisco Bay Area. This was August 1968, and the *San Francisco Examiner* headlines for months had been reporting heavy U.S. casualties from the devastating Tet (New Year) offensive of that same year. Pam had been reading the newspapers and contending with the views of her liberal antiwar professors since her arrival at San Francisco State in the fall of 1965. I knew in her heart she believed I would probably die in Vietnam just as her father had in Korea. Now another war was about to take a man she truly loved, and the pain was more than she could bear. I was too young and too dumb to recognize all the dynamics in Pam concerning the military and war. If I had understood, I probably would have handled things differently.

When I arrived, Pam was standing in front of the huge bay window of her apartment that faced west. From the street, I could see her standing there, watching the late-afternoon sun dip into the Pacific Ocean. Those sunsets had drawn her to the studio apartment several months earlier. Now I could sense she felt the sun setting on her commitment to me. That night was the last time she would let herself love me. As a child, she had learned the lessons well that wars could be costly. The expression on her face when she opened the door imparted the message to me, "I will not love a man who will leave me for a war; it hurts too much."

The evening proved that everything had changed emotionally for the two of us. Our intimacy and trust had been exchanged for the realization that neither of us could control the future. Vietnam had altered our lives without one hostile bullet being fired in our hearing. Not one statistic concerning the war would ever record the pain in each of our hearts. Pam knew I was still a college boy at heart, but she understood instinctively what I would become if I lived through Vietnam. Hand in hand, and yet miles apart in our hearts, we watched the sun disappear into the cool waters of the Pacific. The emotional roller coaster would not come to a stop in either of our lives for many more months. The experience would not reach closure for another year and a half. She would go through Vietnam with me, but it would be at a distance, both physically and emotionally.

My going-away party the following evening helped me change gears by getting Pam off my mind. It was probably the best party the family had ever thrown. The August evening was perfect with the aroma of flowers and fruit trees filling the air. Dad, the true patriarch of the family, was in his glory. My sister, Jan, and her husband, Dewey, had presented Mom and Dad with their first grandson the year before, and then a granddaughter just nine months later. Dad held little Jill like a toy doll and played with his grandson Jeff most of the evening. He and Mom were very happy, enjoying the affection of their grandchildren the entire party.

Food overflowed two long tables on the patio and every aunt and uncle from both sides of the family was in attendance. The family was in full bloom that night. Every member seemed healthy and prosperous and new automobiles lined the street in front of the gathering. At the conclusion of the evening, Dad asked me to cut a large white sheet cake decorated with football and military figures with the words "Best of Luck, Bill" written in blue frosting. Using my Marine Corps sword, I sliced and served each member of the family a piece of the cake. This was more than a dessert. It was a family communion service.

When the evening was over, I met my dad alone in the

living room to thank him for the party. "Thanks, Dad, for the party; it was really great to see everyone," I said.

"Just never forget your family, no matter where you go, and don't forget God either," he admonished me. I let the words go deep into my soul. Coming from my father, a man of few words, they meant something.

Within two weeks, Dad, at age fifty-four, died from a pulmonary embolism. I lost a father, the family lost its patriarch, and nothing would ever be quite the same for any of us. Through my six-month training at the Officers Basic School at Quantico, I continually recalled my father's parting words, "Don't forget your family, and don't forget God either." The months at Quantico, away from the support of family and friends, built a stronger character into me. For the first time in my life, I was without the strength of my father, and the void at times was overwhelming. It all seemed like a nightmare when I thought about the tragic loss. I began to recognize the strength that had been endowed to me through my family. Now, as I was becoming a Marine Corps officer, I was having to learn to stand on my own and lead men. There was little time for grieving.

Although I often felt gutted, a new strength was kicking into action, and I began to call upon it more frequently. I found strength in Sunday chapel services while listening to a highly decorated, combat-veteran chaplain. Something about the man and the way he spoke had caught my attention. I would often be reminded of Dad's final admonition, "Don't forget God either." One Sunday morning after the service was over, I approached the chaplain. With the chapel empty, I stood eye-to-eye with this man of God. "Sir," I began, "I just received orders for Vietnam. I'm an infantry officer, and my father died recently. It's been tough to concentrate these past months, and I don't want to fail my men in combat because of any personal problems."

Without blinking, the chaplain looked deep into my eyes. "Lieutenant," he said with full confidence, "you are to go to Vietnam and lead men because God has something for you there." For a moment, I was speechless. Something powerful in the chaplain's answer made his words seem as though they had come from a source beyond himself.

Finally, I gathered myself and said, "Yes, sir." I felt a new power come into me as I shook the chaplain's battle-scarred hand and whispered, "Thank you, sir." The chaplain, a World War II and Korean War veteran, knew what he had imparted to me. He smiled graciously, turned, and walked out of the chapel. I stood motionless for a moment until the warmth that had poured over me subsided. When I left the chapel that day, I knew that I was on the right path. My destiny awaited me ten thousand miles away in the jungles of Vietnam; my dad had told me not to forget God; and the chaplain had just told me that God had something for me to accomplish. It would be many years before I truly understood what all I had just experienced would mean.

CHAPTER 3

Welcome to Vietnam

The Pan American commercial airliner began what seemed like a nosedive as it quickly lost altitude on its final approach to the Da Nang airport. The bravado of the military personnel that had persisted throughout the flight now gave way to an eerie silence. Young, teenage troops, barely old enough to shave, strained to get their first glimpse of Vietnam through the milky plastic windows of the plane. The approach resembled more of a carnival ride than an aircraft landing. I smiled as the wheels of the aircraft made contact with the runway. It was exactly the way my buddy Gary Nelson had described his own entry into Da Nang in 1966.

The first clue that the plane had indeed landed someplace other than a normal airport was the stench that greeted the men as they descended the ladder and stepped onto the tarmac. "What is that smell?" I asked. Gary had told me about a lot of things I would encounter in Vietnam, but never did he mention the smell. It smelled like a blend of human feces, aviation fuel, and smoldering garbage. The extreme heat and humidity caused the nauseating odor to remain at ground level, nearly suffocating the men as they tried to walk off the tarmac.

The deafening sound of hundreds of artillery pieces blasting away at enemy positions within fifteen miles of

Da Nang was the next hint that the plane hadn't landed in Kansas. The big cannons seemed to be talking to one another as they fired round after round into the distant jungles and rice paddies. While staring at the lush mountains southwest of the airfield, I stood motionless and listened to the big guns bark. A Phantom jet roared down the runway to the north, gray smoke pouring from its engines. It reminded me of the dragsters at the Freemont Raceway. My buddy, Lee Wallace, and I used to crowd the finish line to watch the big rail jobs whiz by so fast they needed huge parachutes to bring them to a stop. As the Phantom lifted off the runway and banked hard right with its engines screaming, I was reminded that Lee was now flying one of them for the Marine Corps. The question came into my mind: How does Lee handle a Phantom jet when he could barely keep his '57 Ford on the road? I shook my head and moved off the tarmac and into a small terminal.

A few moments later, I exited the terminal carrying my seabag. I climbed into a military vehicle bound for the 1st Marine Division (a.k.a. 1st MarDiv) located on Hill 327, three miles to the east. Along the way, I saw what you might expect to see in any country devastated by decades of war. Refugees had built shanty villages that lined both sides of the road for miles. Children seemed to greatly outnumber the adult Vietnamese population, and hundreds of kids wandered alongside the road, begging, but still able to smile and wave as the truck rushed by them. Children are so resilient. Although those little ones had been displaced by the war, they seemed well fed. Their clothes were shabby, but their eyes were alive with the mischief that fills all children's hearts. I began to understand why they had warned my fellow officers and me that children in Vietnam could be alluring but sometimes very lethal. They seemed so innocent, and most of them probably were. But it only took one bad kid to ruin your day or your life with a well-placed booby trap. Quickly, I was reminded that I was in Vietnam for a war, called to serve in the Marine Corps, not the Peace Corps.

Everything seemed to be moving quickly. The hurry-up-and-wait days of training were obviously behind me. Every step of the process of joining the 1st Marine Division was quick and efficient. From the G-3 administration to the supply guys who issued my first pair of jungle utilities, everything went well. The constant sound of outgoing artillery blasts didn't allow me one minute to forget where I was. Finally the pace slowed as I approached the division briefing room. Its plyboard sides belched with the concussion from the cannons. The tin roof lifted slightly, almost like a salute, each time the big guns fired. I stared straight ahead, directly into the eyes of the briefing officer. He was Marine captain Charles Robb, the son-in-law of former president Lyndon Baines Johnson. Robb's face had graced every newspaper, TV program, and magazine of any significance since his marriage to LBJ's daughter. To his credit, Robb had married Linda Bird Johnson at the height of the controversy over the war. This guy must love trouble, I thought as I studied Robb's every move. His polish, confidence, and notable quiet humility impressed me.

The briefing was clear and concise. The 1st Marine Division was taking a lot of casualties. This was all I could glean from Robb's briefing. The words "were killed" echoed across the room each time he said them. The authority of those words carried a greater impact than the black, bold headlines of the *San Francisco Examiner* report on the war's weekly body count. The count had peaked in 1968. Those numbers were chilling, and actual battlefield footage of Vietnam had become the companion of the nightly TV network news. But none of that could touch the intensity that I felt in my gut as I heard about the casualties firsthand.

Captain Robb switched gears in his presentation from the overall strategic level of the Marine Corps responsibility for the war. He began to talk about the tactical level. Once again, the word *killed* became operative as Robb gave a blow-by-blow description of the activities of the 1st Marine Division's Battalion and Force Recon units. I sat up a little straighter as Robb laid out the situation that the two recon units were facing. Force Recon had been the division's deep reconnaissance capability, while Battalion Recon worked in much closer to friendly units. Information-gathering five-day patrols in enemy-controlled areas were the reconnaissance missions in a nutshell. There had been heavy contact with enemy troops and "Two lieutenants from 1st Force Recon have been killed," Robb reported. Without looking up, he growled, "Do I have any volunteers for 1st Force?" My hand shot up. Robb made immediate eye contact with me as though he knew exactly where to look in the sea of faces. "Your name, Lieutenant, and your service number," he said quietly. Once again he dropped his eyes to the papers in front of him. "Lt. Bill Peters 0107112" was my reply. With that brief exchange came an overwhelming sense of destiny.

By 1969, the H-34 helicopter had nearly outlived its usefulness in the Vietnam War. I had heard all the horror stories about them, hunks of metal that resembled a fat grasshopper with one propeller on its head and the other on its tail. "Is this thing going to make it to An Hoa?" was my main question as the ancient 34 shook and rattled its way west from the coast city of Da Nang. Hell, I thought, what a waste it would be getting killed in one of these pieces of crap. Is this thing going to stay in the air? How far have we gone? My mind raced; my adrenaline peaked as the chopper started its descent into the hot, dusty An Hoa Valley. I was slapped by the unbearable heat and dust, and the scream of the ancient chopper's engine sounded like it was about to come apart. This was just a drumroll for the impact of the bird's shock absorbers and hard rubber tires against the white-hot metal runway.

"Get out, get out, Lieutenant. Hurry up; we gotta get out of here; we're taking fire; move it, Lieutenant!" hollered the 34's wild-eyed crew chief. Just as I jumped from the side door of the besieged bird, I heard a loud crack, like the sound of a bullwhip. Out of the corner of my eye, I saw the crew chief clutching his thigh. Blood gushed from a single gunshot wound that had torn through the leg of his green jungle utilities. I lay facedown on the metal runway. The chopper hovered above me for a few seconds, struggling to gain power while trying to escape the enemy's automatic-weapon fire, while the door gunner on the beleaguered bird blasted back. He sprayed M-60 machinegun fire in the direction of some muzzle flashes coming from a small knoll above the airstrip. I took advantage of the chopper's cover fire, rose to my feet, grabbed my gear, and ran toward a bunker at the edge of the runway. By that time, I was soaked in my own sweat. Every pore of my body gushed forth as I sprinted toward the bunker. I dove over a wall of sandbags surrounding the bunker, quickly checking to make sure the fluid pouring from my body was not blood. When nothing red appeared against the backdrop of my green uniform, my eyes went heavenward as I breathed a silent thank-you.

"Welcome to the Nam, Lieutenant," said a voice from the bunker. I looked up to see the snaggle-toothed grin of a kid who looked no older than seventeen. "Man, we was bettin' you was gonna get nailed by that AK-47 fire. Hell, three of them rounds looked like they bit your butt," the young Marine said. I didn't want to know how close I had come, so I immediately changed the subject by asking where the 1st Force Recon Company compound was located. I barely got the question out of my mouth when a voice inside the bunker shouted, "Incoming!" I had no time to react. I just rolled over onto my stomach, buried my face into the ground, covering my head with my hands and arms. The Russian-made rocket whistled over the top of the bunker and impacted about one hundred yards to the north. The crack of the metal casing around the rocket reverberated as it exploded, sending shrapnel in every direction. I raised my head after a moment, only to encounter the snaggle-toothed Marine grinning at me from the bunker.

"Lieutenant, do ya see where that rocket landed? Well, sir, that's the 1st Force Recon compound. Just follow the smoke," the young Marine said while pointing.

I no sooner began to walk in the direction of the smoke than two troop transport CH-46 helicopters swooped out of the sky, both making hard landings on the metal runway. The 46s were a step up from the 34 that had just deposited me on the runway. Force Recon Marines, looking like gunfighters right out of the Wild West, poured down the rear ramp of one of the choppers. The pilots and crew chief followed the recon teams onto the tarmac, congratulating them and pointing to dozens of bullet holes that laced the back of their aircraft. I dropped my gear and approached a scene that reminded me of football players reliving the action of a big game. I had done it hundreds of times during many seasons playing that sport. There seemed to be a healthy camaraderie among the salty-looking Force Recon troops. It was my first time in such a setting that I was without my buddy Lee. I really missed him as I watched the recon team sharing the obvious victory of the moment. I instantly felt a part of those muddy, sweaty, skinny, subhuman, happy misfits who were growling like wild animals.

The thing that really impressed me was how quickly the sniper fire had ceased when the recon team landed. I was ignored as I stood in the midst of this fraternity of men as they talked about their last five days of patrolling as a six-man team, deep in enemy-controlled territory. They had not spoken above a whisper for days, and now their emotions were exploding in one another's faces. They had eaten together, slept inches apart, observed each other's hand signals, and often tried to read one another's minds. But for days, they had not been able to share their feelings or frustrations. Now they could talk as loud and long as they wanted. They laughed and chided, but treated each other with an unspoken respect that only men who have shared a life-or-death experience could appreciate. They were young but looked aged and ragged. A shower, shave, and a good meal would transform them into the magnificent-looking gunfighters and Marines they really were. I finally took advantage of a lull in the celebration and introduced myself to the man who appeared to be the recon team leader. His name was Lt. Wayne Rollings, and he looked to be in his late twenties. He spoke with a southern drawl and represented himself as a new addition to the 1st Force Reconnaissance Company. Rollings looked me over and wiped the sweat out of his eyes, smearing the green camouflage paint across the back of his right hand. I couldn't help notice that the little finger and ring finger on his right hand were missing. Trying not to stare at his hand, I quickly made eye contact and spoke up: "I'm reporting into 1st Force. Can I get a ride with your team over to the compound?"

"Sure, Peters," Rollings responded. "The truck will be picking us up pretty quick." Aware that I would soon be part of the 1st Force family, Rollings began to share the events of the last five days of patrolling in an area he referred to as Base Area 112. "Yeah, we crashed one chopper on the insert. It just sorta rolled over on its side in the LZ. We made sure the pilot and crew were picked up before we began our mission. The chopper caught fire and blew up, letting the enemy know we were in the area," Rollings continued. I found out as we talked that Rollings had been an enlisted Marine, rising to the rank of sergeant. After returning to the University of Georgia on a track and football scholarship, he graduated and took a Marine Corps commission. I remembered Rollings from Officers Candidate School and the Basic School at Quantico. Although he might have been new to Vietnam, he seemed like a seasoned vet. He had plenty of command experience from his enlisted days in the Corps, and that gave him immediate respect from his men.

Rollings did not hesitate to introduce me to the other recon Marines. There was Sergeant Mckee, a tough-talking, cocky kid who could not have weighed 130 pounds dripping wet. He had fifty patrols under his belt over an eighteen-month tour. Sergeant Morin had a choirboy's looks and deep scars on his neck from a bullet wound that nearly took his life during his first Vietnam tour in 1965. You could tell that Rollings and the two sergeants were the main players on the team. The rest of the men were taking their cues from them and were like a supporting cast to those stars.

I learned a lot about 1st Force from this conversation with Rollings. During the truck ride to the compound, I learned even more about the company's mission. First Force and its 160 men were the eyes and ears for the

10,000-man 1st Marine Division. The division's tactical area of responsibility stretched from Hue City to the north and then east to Da Nang. From there, it extended west to the Laotian border and south to Chu Lai. The III Marine Amphibious Force not only oversaw that area but also commanded the 3d Marine Division, whose troops stretched from Hue City north to the Demilitarized Zone and west to the Laotian border, all in all a huge, mountainous tactical area of responsibility. The role of 1st Force Recon, as the eyes and ears of the 1st Marine Division, had become crucial. There were rumors that President Nixon was about to announce that American troops were preparing to withdraw from Vietnam, and 1st Force's work, in enemy-controlled territory, had become vital to reporting any large North Vietnamese Army buildups. The small recon teams had the ability to call for massive air strikes against enemy troop concentrations and base camps hidden deep in the mountains of the Central Highlands. This had proved very successful in keeping the North Vietnamese troops off balance. First Force was normally an intelligence-gathering unit, but recently its six- and eight-man teams had become "tactical" by engaging the North Vietnamese Army with ambushes and prisoner grabs, and by calling in fixed-wing air strikes. The enemy hated their guts and relentlessly pursued the recon teams when they discovered them patrolling their base camp areas.

The same afternoon Rollings and I met on the hot, dusty airstrip at An Hoa, another very significant meeting was taking place two hundred miles to the south. This was a political meeting that was being held by the U.S. secretary of defense, Melvin Laird, and Gen. Creighton Abrams, the commanding general of MACV, the top command overseeing the war in Vietnam. Laird had been sent by President Richard Nixon to Vietnam on an official fact-finding mission. Laird's visit was to have a profound effect on the primary mission of 1st Force Reconnaissance Company because Laird shocked General Abrams with the news that the president felt it was time to turn the war over to South Vietnam. It was apparent to Abrams and his staff during the course of the Laird visit that there was little to be done in the area of fact finding. Laird and Nixon had made up their minds. Laird's intention was to give the impression that he came to take a strategic look at the war. Then on his return he could announce that it was time to turn the war over to our Vietnamese allies.

Abrams then met with his corps commanders, including General Nickerson, the commanding general of all Marine forces in Vietnam. Abrams told his supporting commanders that the secretary of defense would soon announce the beginning of the withdrawal of U.S. troops from South Vietnam. Recognizing that turning the war over to the South Vietnamese forces would make his own troops more vulnerable, General Nickerson informed Abrams that he would need a better strategic and operational intelligence collection effort in order to ensure the security of I Corps during the withdrawal.

"The well is dry, Herman," Abrams responded. "You'll have to do it out of your own hide. I have no intelligence forces to provide you." Abrams advised Nickerson and the other corps commanders that they would have to cover the loss of troops with a better reconnaissance support effort that did not rely on the assets of MACV. Nickerson immediately recognized that the burden of his reconnaissance screen would now be placed squarely on the shoulders of 1st Force Reconnaissance Company and her sister company, 3d Force Reconnaissance, located to the north. It would, however, take several months to activate 3d Force, so 1st Force would have to get the job done. With the first withdrawals scheduled to begin immediately, the role of 1st Force Recon would become even more crucial to the Marine forces that were deployed from the DMZ south to the Central Highlands.

General Nickerson returned to his headquarters in Da Nang. Nickerson immediately convened his staff and subordinate commanders, including Maj. Roger Simmons, 1st Force Recon's flamboyant company commander, and proceeded to tell them that the United States had reached a pivotal juncture in the war.

After dropping the withdrawal bombshell on General Abrams, Secretary of Defense Laird prepared to leave Saigon immediately and return to Washington, D.C. He was planning to make an important announcement when he stepped onto the tarmac at Andrews Air Force Base. Euphoric over his fact-finding mission and without discussing his intentions with President Nixon, the commander in chief, he was about to tell the American people that the withdrawal of American forces from South Vietnam was imminent.

Nickerson didn't tell his subordinates that Secretary Laird and President Nixon had their minds made up before the so-called fact-finding mission even began. He chose, instead, to point out that the withdrawal would usher in the most vulnerable phase of the Vietnam War. Looking directly at Major Simmons, he stated emphatically, "The burdens will be greater, particularly for reconnaissance units."

A six-by transport truck skidded to a stop in front of the 1st Force command bunker, kicking up a huge cloud of dust to envelop the recon Marines sitting in the open back.

The men jumped to the ground with a growl and walked off toward a couple of rows of large, hard-backed tents lining the compound. Rollings and I headed toward the command bunker, a heavily sandbagged structure about ten feet high, thirty feet long, and twenty feet wide with a few aerials poking from its roof. The sound of friendly artillery fire shook the bunker. Seeing the uncertainty in my eyes, Rollings pointed south and said, "All the commotion comes from our 175 guns right over there. You'll get used to it." Just as we approached the door of the bunker, a tall, muscular Marine major was exiting. Rollings and I raised a salute, which was expected in the safety of the compound. The major returned the salute as Rollings greeted him and introduced me as the new lieutenant reporting in to take Lieutenant Slater's place. "Major Simmons, sir, it's good to meet you, sir."

The major shook my hand and said, "Good to have you aboard, Lieutenant." Simmons had recently returned from his meeting with General Nickerson at III MAF and acted genuinely pleased to have a new officer assigned to his company. "You get the lieutenant checked in, and I'll see you at chow," the major said while nodding at Rollings. "Oh, by the way, you and your team owe the air wing a half million dollars for the chopper you caused them to lose on your insert. They said you chose a poor landing zone," the major said. I was almost positive he was joking.

"No, sir, that LZ was perfect; we just took a lot of AK-47 fire on the way in, and I think we lost our hydraulics," Rollings explained.

" 'Hydraulics,' Lieutenant? You're starting to sound like one of those wing guys." The major flashed a broad grin.

A smoky haze and odor filled the 1st Force compound. Rollings and I, weighted down with our gear, walked slowly toward the officers' tent. As we approached a section of the camp near the airstrip, we stopped to gaze upon a shredded ten-by-twenty-foot green tent with a smoldering wooden floor. "That was where you were going to be sacking out. I guess we've only got one officers' tent now. Damn rocket must of blown it away. Come on with me," Rollings said, motioning to me. A few feet away stood a tent that had not been touched by the rocket. Rollings threw open the flap and boldly walked in while unbuckling his web belt and allowing his gear to crash against the plyboard floor. Four Marines squinted to see who had come into the dimly lit tent. "Damn," Rollings roared, "let's get some light and air in here."

"Razor, is that you, bro?" The voice came from one of the racks in the back of the tent.

"Damn right it's me," Rollings replied. Razor was Rollings's nickname, and it seemed very fitting. "I brought Slater's replacement; I want you to meet Bill Peters." While Rollings started pulling up the sides of the tent, a couple of the previously shadowy figures began to take shape and move in my direction.

"Welcome aboard, Peters, I'm Lynn Lowder." Lowder, a six-foot-five midwesterner, stuck out his large hand to greet me. Then he began to introduce the other lieutenants, who were sizing me up from different areas of the tent. "Peters, this is Ric Miller," Lowder said. He pointed to a smirking Marine sitting at a bar made of wooden ammo crates. Miller was sipping a warm can of Carling's Black Label beer. Miller acknowledged me by hoisting the can in my direction and nodding his head. At age twenty-one, Miller already had four years in Vietnam. His boyish looks and personality were just a veneer covering a consummate warrior that had fought from one end of Vietnam to the other. Miller had seen it all, and now he was at 1st Force Recon, the Marine Corps' most elite unit, because he wanted to cap off his final tour with as much action as he could find or create.

Lowder introduced another Marine, who barely looked up from cleaning his weapon. "Randy Champe, this is Bill Peters." Champe's head moved slightly as his eyes rolled upward to meet my glance. "Randy, Randy, Randy, hammer, hammer, hammer, saw, saw, saw, you are always so damn busy, Randy, Randy," Miller sang. Then came what the other recon lieutenants referred to as "the grin." Champe communicated a lot with that grin.

Bob Hansen, the company's communications officer, stuck his head into the tent. Hansen, a graduate of the University of New Mexico, was a classmate of Champe's, who was also a New Mexico alumnus. "Randy, let's go get some chow, bro," Hansen shouted.

"Bob, come on in and meet Bill Peters, Slater's replacement," Lowder said as he pulled Hansen into the tent. Every time Slater's name was mentioned, I noticed an uneasy look among my new compatriots. Obviously something tragic had happened to my predecessor, but just then was not the time to ask, I thought. A shadowy figure in the rear of the tent rolled his legs off a cot onto the floor and then sat up. Lynn identified this thin, red-headed, freckle-faced Marine as Jim Ritchie, another Californian, who had graduated from the University of California at Berkley in 1968. Ritchie managed to raise his hand to acknowledge me.

After Hansen and Champe left the tent, the other lieutenants began to straighten up their appearances before they all filed out and headed for the chow hall located a couple of hundred meters away at the artillery battery, just across a wire barricade next to the airstrip. The walk could have been either dusty or muddy, depending on the weather. That day it was dusty and hot. Champe, Hansen, and Miller were all first lieutenants, while Lowder, Rollings, Ritchie, and myself were still second—better known as brown-bar—lieutenants. But there did not seem to be any recognition of rank among them, and whatever had happened to Slater was not keeping them from welcoming me into their obviously tight-knit group. The lieutenants headed straight for some tin-roofed buildings they referred to as hootches that were right next to a battery of huge artillery pieces, and the big 175 guns were thundering as they sent payloads up to twelve miles into the mountains that loomed above the An Hoa Valley. The tin-roofed mess hall belonged to the artillery battery, and we Force Recon Marines were their guests. During each fire mission, the mess hootch shook from the shock waves that the big guns released.

We'd no sooner started through the chow line than an enemy mortar round impacted in the artillery battery compound, sending shrapnel, smoke, and dust through the mess hootch. Instantly, every Marine hit the deck, dumping food and drinks all over each other as instincts and training sent them flat on their bellies. A second round landed a little closer to the mess hall, and a piece of hot twisted metal ripped through the one-inch pine wall. Jumping to our feet, we all ran toward the door of the hootch. Obviously, the enemy was walking the mortars in on the mess hall, because the second explosion was closer than the first. We ran like hell, then dived into the first available sandbagged bunker. The next mortar round landed within twenty meters of the mess hall, ripping a hole in the roof. Then one more mortar round slammed into the compound, but that one was so close to the hall that the concussion caused one of the walls to buckle completely. Part of the roof crashed into the kitchen.

Suddenly the Marine artillery battery began a fire mission so violent that it shook the ground like an earthquake. "That's it," someone announced, "our guns are on the enemy position, so let's get the hell out of here while we have the chance." We moved out of the bunker and sprinted for our compound, about two hundred meters to the northeast. Picking up the pace as we moved out, we refused to even look over our shoulders at the destruction that could have taken our lives.

As we approached the 1st Force compound, we saw Major Simmons and his executive officer, Capt. Dal Williams, standing in front of the command bunker. Both were wearing broad grins. Slowing our pace from a sprint to a jog, we approached the senior officers. Major Simmons motioned us to come over and join him and Captain Williams. We raised our salutes in unison as Simmons and Williams reciprocated. I think there were only three of us that had wound up running away from the mess hootch together. I learned that some of the other lieutenants hadn't even made it to the chow line when the attack came. They were the first ones back to the 1st Force compound. "In a hurry, men? Was the food that bad that you decided to burn down the mess hall?" Simmons said. Motioning to me, he said, "Looks like a couple of you got more chow on your utilities than in your stomach. You're gonna be eating C rations in your tent while they clean up that catastrophe." Captain Williams couldn't contain himself and burst into peals of uncontrollable laughter. In his late twenties, Williams was a California boy with a football player's body but a tennis player's heart. He was a 1962 graduate of Sacramento State College, where he lettered four times in tennis. He was on his second tour in Vietnam. Williams had paid his dues as a platoon leader his first tour, and the other lieutenants liked and respected him as an older brother. Williams chuckled as he made a backhand motion with an imaginary tennis racket in the direction of the artillery battery compound. "I'd say the NVA won that match." It was not what Williams said but the way he said it that made us crack up with laughter. Williams was cool but totally competent. When two Recon Marines were drowned during an ill-fated cable-ladder extract out of Base Area 112, it was Williams who returned with a reaction force and scuba gear to recover their bodies.

I studied Major Simmons and Captain Williams as they continued their conversation with the other officers. I felt a sense of strong leadership in the two Marines. Williams asked me what part of the country I was from. "California, sir."

Showing an interest in the new guy, he asked, "What part of California?"

"San Francisco Bay Area, sir," I replied.

"Where did you go to school?" Williams said.

"San Francisco State, sir."

With a menacing smile, Williams repeated, "San Francisco State, oh yeah, that's the hippie school, isn't it?"

"All the colleges are hippie schools now, Captain," I countered.

"Not my beloved Sac State," Williams said.

"Sacramento State may be the last bastion of conservatism, but San Francisco kicked their football team's ass last year, which isn't bad for a bunch of hippies, sir," I added with a cooky grin.

Major Simmons quickly turned the whole conversation into business, which he was a master at doing. Simmons was one of the original team leaders chosen for Force Recon when the unit was created in the 1950s. He ranked at the top of his class at the famous British Commando School. The lieutenants knew if Simmons asked them to do something, that it was not something that he couldn't do himself. Once Simmons had our attention, he announced, "I want you in the briefing tent tonight at 1900 for a meeting."

Almost in cadence, the lieutenants replied, "Yes, sir." With that we saluted and walked off toward our tent.

We had no sooner returned to the officers' tent than two more CH-46 helicopters landed off the airstrip near the 1st Force compound. Lowder lifted the flap of the tent and squinted through a pair of binoculars at the choppers. "It's Hostage Hog's team and, man, does the Hog look pissed," Lowder announced. Lieutenant Brodder, a former college football player, had earned the nickname Hostage Hog because of his lineman's build and immense appetite for junk food. The Hog had been asked to do the impossible by conducting a mission that was considered very dangerous, even by Force Recon standards. His mission was to locate the headquarters in the I Corps area for the North Vietnamese Army's highest command group, known by the code name "Front Four." This was said to be an elite cadre of generals who supposedly had defeated the French at Dien Bien Phu. Now Front Four moved in and out of jungle sanctuaries along the Laotian and Cambodian borders, with the mission of driving the Americans out of South Vietnam.

The cloud of dust from the choppers reached the entrance to the lieutenant's tent about the same time as Hostage Hog, who threw open the tent's canvas door and stood there in a haze. Ric gave the formal greeting: "Hog, how you doing, buddy? Get in here and have a beer."

Hog grabbed a warm beer out of the lifeless old refrigerator and chugged it down. The excess foam ran down his chin, turning into a stream of mud as it rolled down his neck. Brodder was totally stressed as he began to mumble,

"They wouldn't let us get on the ground. Hell, there was so much small-arms fire in the LZ, you would have thought they knew we were coming."

Ric dropped his happy-go-lucky attitude and became deadly serious. "I was checking out the routing of my operations order, and lo and behold, guess whose name was included?" Ric said.

"Who cares about the routing?" Hog countered.

"You better start caring, because the chief of Duc Duc Province is getting a copy of each of our operations orders, and he has been known as a VC sympathizer for years. When I was in the grunts, we used to have all kinds of trouble with Duc Duc," Ric continued.

Hog reached for another warm beer and chugged it down in record time. "That's it, I'm transferring to the grunts; I can't take this crap anymore. That's it, no more!" Hog yelled at the top of his lungs. "I gotta have the firepower of a platoon to do the job I came here to do. This taking on companies and battalions of NVA with eight Marines ain't cuttin' it," Hog finished with a whisper. Realizing how fried Hog really was, Ric said, "You're right about that, buddy. Going after Front Four head-on could wipe out a recon team real quick."

The rest of the lieutenants agreed either orally or with a nod of the head. I didn't say anything; I was just trying to take it all in. This had been my day of baptism by fire. I had gotten off the chopper just three hours earlier at An Hoa, where I had been chased off the metal airstrip with AK-47 rounds nipping at my heels. Within seconds, a Russian-made 122 rocket had taken out the tent I would have been sleeping in, and the mess hall where I had tried to have dinner got hit by NVA mortars. Now I was witnessing a discussion about some group of enemy generals called Front Four, who seemed to be bigger than life itself. I thought to myself, If this is day one, what can I expect the rest of the year to be like?

There was dead quiet in the briefing tent as the lieutenants sat on metal folding chairs arranged in classroom fashion. In front of them hung a large blackboard and a map of 1st Force's tactical area of responsibility.

Captain Williams brought the lieutenants to attention as Major Simmons entered the tent. "Good evening, men, at ease, take your seats," the major ordered with an air of professionalism. "Welcome back, Lieutenant Brodder. Sorry we couldn't get you into that area. However, it works well for you because your request for an infantry platoon has been granted. You will be reporting to 1st Marines tomorrow at 0800. Ed, the best of luck to you," Simmons said. A look of relief came over Hostage Hog's face as he realized that his suicide mission had been canceled. Men came and went in Force Recon, but Hog would be missed; he was special.

Major Simmons continued speaking. "It isn't often that all you men are in from the bush at the same time, so while I got all of you here, I want to brief you on a few things. We will no longer be under the operational control of the division. From now on, we will be under the operational control of the III Marine Amphibious Force. This means the stakes will be much higher, and the nature of the missions will be more along the lines of what Lieutenant Brodder was just engaged in. MAF wants us rattling the 2d NVA Division's cage, and that means locating and harassing the hell out of them."

Ric straightened up in his chair, leaned forward, raised his head, and said, "Sir?" When Simmons acknowledged him, Miller said with some authority, "Major, when I was in the Combined Action Platoon, we learned the chief of Duc Duc Province was a real Viet Cong sympathizer. I recommend that none of our operation orders be routed to him."

Simmons nodded. "I'll check into that, Lieutenant Miller, and if it's still true, we will deal with it."

Simmons began to read from his big yellow, legal-size notepad. In unison, the lieutenants reached for their Marine Corps–issue platoon leader notepads. I observed the soberness of the group somewhat as an outsider, but already in my heart, I felt a part of them. The major systematically went through a list of instructions that included the manning of defensive positions each night. He informed Lieutenant Rollings that his next mission would be a prisoner acquisition and that I would accompany him on that patrol. The major was wasting no time in getting the new guy snapped in and operational. Rollings waited until the major closed the yellow notepad before he made eye contact with me. Then, as Captain Williams called the lieutenants to attention, Rollings motioned to me that he wanted to talk. I nodded to Rollings as the major bid the lieutenants a good evening and left the tent.

Rollings and I met at the back of the tent. "Bill, I get my op order tomorrow morning. We'll have a meeting with my men around noon and go over all the details of the mission. You need to get all your gear issued to you. I'll show you what to take to the field." What he didn't share with me was the integral role in the prisoner grab the new lieutenant would play.

The lieutenants headed back to their tent, checking on their platoons on the way. I followed Rollings and observed how he related with his men. The team of dusty, dirty Marines that I had met on the airstrip early that afternoon had been transformed into a spit-and-polish, squared-away outfit. Their heads were shaved, and their utilities and boots were spotless. Sergeant Mckee brought

the team to attention as Rollings and I entered the tent.
Although these men represented 6th Platoon, they didn't
resemble the size or nature of an infantry platoon. The
infantry platoon carried nearly thirty men, while Force
Recon platoons were about half that size. The discipline
of these troops was evident. They were mature beyond
their years. Rollings addressed the team. "Men, we got a
prisoner grab coming up here in the next couple of days.
I should have the operation order tomorrow morning.
Sergeant Mckee and I will discuss it, and then we will be
briefing you. Get a good night's sleep, but remember—if
we get hit tonight with mortars or rockets, you will man
the west perimeter. You will need to be wearing helmets
and flak jackets." With those instructions, Rollings and I
left the platoon and headed for the lieutenants' tent.

I spent a restless night. Outgoing artillery fire rocked
the tent, hour after hour. At about midnight, friendly artillery, mortars, machine-gun fire, and flares lit up the
compound. I jumped to my feet and started to reach for my
flak jacket and helmet. "Relax," came a voice from one of
the cots on the other side of the tent, "it's only one of our
time-on-targets. We throw everything we've got at them
for a few minutes just to let them know we ain't all
sleeping."

"Oh," I replied as I lay back down. The odor of gunpowder and the smell of burnt canvas from the remnants
of the neighboring tent filled the air. The humidity, noise,
and foul smells were a constant reminder to me, that first
night in Vietnam.

CHAPTER 4

Snapping In

The preparation for the prisoner grab went swiftly. Rollings led me through the steps of preparation for a recon patrol. Sergeant Mckee was key as a liaison between Rollings and the rest of the team. The lieutenant gave the order, and Mckee followed through on every detail. The sergeant couldn't have been more than twenty-one years old. He had fifty patrols under his belt and as many kills while running point on the majority of those missions. He didn't talk about where he came from. His conversation always started in Vietnam and ended there. It was as though he had never had another life. Two years in country had transformed that young warrior from high-school kid to killer, and there didn't seem to be any turning back for him. He had become a machine that focused on preparation and survival. Nothing slipped by him. If one of the Marine's pieces of equipment rattled, Sergeant Mckee silenced it with green tape. If his skin was shiny or white, Sergeant Mckee smeared black camouflage paint on it. He made the team jump up and down in their full-field gear. He listened for any human sound that would give them away in the jungle to the savvy North Vietnamese Army. Every detail had to be perfect before he reported to Rollings for the final inspection.

On this, my first patrol, I became the brunt of an old

Force Recon tradition. I was loaded down with all the extra ammunition for Sergeant Morin's M-60 machine gun. Extra M-79 high-explosive grenade launcher rounds were also thrown in for good measure. My equipment easily weighed over one hundred pounds. For that mission, the tradition should have been dropped, because I was also assigned the responsibility of grabbing the prisoner. As the new lieutenant, I welcomed the challenge. I accepted the extra weight and my role in the grab without a question; it was my first mission, and I wanted to pay my dues quickly. I knew that if I performed well under fire I would be accepted into the brotherhood. At that point in my Marine Corps career, that meant more to me than life itself.

The whine of the big CH-46 troop transport was deafening as we flew west toward the Laotian border. Rollings had chosen his best men for this very dangerous mission. Sergeant Mckee sat close to the tailgate of the chopper, ready to follow his leader down the ramp once the bird had landed. If the chopper wasn't challenged after a few seconds in the LZ, then the rear ramp would be slowly lowered. Inserting a team into enemy-controlled territory that way was as close to a World War II beach landing as a Marine Corps unit in Vietnam could get. The lieutenant or team leader was always the first man to go down the ramp, which was always one of the most dangerous moments of the mission. The NVA knew this tactic and often held their fire until the first man left the chopper. Then they would open up, trying to kill the leader of the patrol. Rollings stood up, pointed to his M-16 rifle, and cranked a round into the chamber. I followed suit, along with the rest of the team. Then Rollings pointed down, signaling that they were over the LZ. Sergeant Morin slammed a round into the chamber of the big M-60 machine gun and rested the weapon's muzzle outboard on one of the open oval port-holes of the chopper. I was taking my cues from Rollings and the others. The patrol was on-the-job training for this new lieutenant, and I knew that my life depended on how quickly I learned.

The CH-46 spiraled in tight turns toward earth to lose altitude for landing. Its sister ship began to circle off in the distance, ready to swoop in and bail the team out if we got on the ground and came under heavy attack. Huey helicopter gunships made their final passes over the LZ and sprayed it with machine-gun fire. As the CH-46 began to quickly lose altitude, the pressure on the legs of the recon team nearly welded each of us to our positions. To lift our legs and walk was a real effort as the big bird made its final descent into the landing zone. The Marines occupied every open port in the chopper, eyes scanning the dense jungle foliage surrounding the LZ. Dust and debris on the jungle floor were stirred up by the prop blast of the twin-engine chopper as it touched down. I watched Rollings and Mckee carefully move down the ramp as it was lowered. They stood motionless a few feet from the rear of the chopper. When they had been on the ground for a few seconds, they signaled for the rest of the team to follow them off the chopper.

The team disappeared into the jungle as the chopper lifted out of the LZ, gained altitude, and pulled up over the tall jungle canopy. The team headed north for a couple of minutes before Rollings gave the signal to halt and form a perimeter. I watched as Rollings and the radioman moved to the middle of the perimeter. Rollings whispered into the handset of the radio, giving Major Simmons and the operations officer in the 1st Force command bunker at An Hoa the team's position. To distinguish it from any other traffic on that radio frequency, the team's call sign for that patrol was Lunch Meat. Rollings signaled me to move in next to him as he made his report. Every important part of the report was coded. The team's grid coordinates, direction of travel, and current halted status were all being read by Rollings from a coded crib sheet. Rollings whispered to me, "Watch everything I do, and if the crap hits the fan, stick close to me." I answered Rollings with a simple thumbs-up.

Sergeant Mckee took the point while Sergeant Morin assumed the deuce point with the M-60 machine gun on his hip. Rollings and then the main radioman came next, with me and the secondary radioman following them. The position of the last man in the patrol was known as tail-end Charlie. This vital rearguard position had been filled just an hour before the patrol stepped on the chopper at An Hoa. Sgt. Eugene Ayers, a salty thirty-three-year-old vet, had just reported the day before to 1st Force, and because of his depth of experience in Vietnam, he had been able to lobby Simmons into sending him on the patrol. Ayers's snaggle-toothed grin and sincere eyes were a dead give-away that beneath the camouflage paint there was a real human being. He was short and pudgy, but he moved like a panther through the thick jungle. Only the secondary radioman was between me and Ayers, so I could observe the precision with which Ayers operated as he covered the patrol's route. Ayers straightened and replaced vegetation, dusted out the team's boot prints with tree branches, and walked backward most of the time. He would vanish from time to time, and then quietly reappear behind the radioman as though he were a ghost. I was learning through Ayers what a work of art a good tail-end Charlie could be. Ayers was also a great backup team leader because he knew his limitations. He had reassured Major Simmons that he wasn't interested in being a team leader. He just wanted to be someone's platoon sergeant and run tail-end Charlie.

The jungle was very quiet once the chopper had left. Too quiet. I could tell Ayers didn't like what he sensed. Skillfully, he continued to cover Lunch Meat's movements, sometimes falling back as much as fifty meters to listen, watch, and make sure we were not being followed. Ayers wondered if it was the scent and movement of the Americans that had caused such a hush in the jungle; the only other thing it could be, he whispered to Rollings, was "NVA, and lots of them." Ayers's eyes and ears strained to pick up any human sound. Then we started up the mountain that stood between us and our objective, a well-traveled, high-speed trail in the valley to the north. Rollings periodically stopped the patrol for a rest, allowing Ayers to catch up. Finally Ayers solved the mystery as to the silence that was so contrary to the usually noisy jungle bird sanctuary. Hundreds of NVA were moving parallel to the team on a trail hidden from the air by three-hundred-foot-high jungle canopy. Ayers had gotten the break he needed when he scaled a rock hanging over a huge draw. About two hundred meters below him, he could see the enemy as they moved through a forty-meter-long bombed-out area before melting back into the jungle. A less experienced Marine would not have picked up on this, but Ayers knew the bush and always looked for enemy movement across any clearing or bombed-out area. The NVA were moving briskly, which meant they felt secure that no one was in the area. Ayers put the binoculars to his eyes, bringing the enemy into focus. He began to count under his breath as he studied their weapons and equipment. After he had observed well over a hundred NVA, he began to make notes in his patrol notebook. The crafty old sergeant, pro that he was, refused to commit any of it to memory because he understood that this was just the first few hours of a possible five-day patrol. But knowing where the enemy was located at least released Ayers to move a little more swiftly to catch up with the team.

The secondary radioman looked startled as Ayers gently placed his hand on the young Marine's shoulder to get his attention. Ayers then took the handset and whispered in it. The primary radioman picked up Ayers's voice and immediately signaled Rollings, who stopped the team with the clenched fist that meant freeze. Sergeant Mckee's heart raced as his thumb moved into position to release the safety on his weapon. Sergeant Morin moved the muzzle of the M-60 to cover Mckee's left flank. Rollings pressed the handset to the radio hard against his ear to hear Ayers. My eyes moved back and forth from Ayers to Rollings while I tried to read their lips. The suspense was incredible. Finally, a faint smile crossed Rollings's lips. He gave the signal to drop down on one knee. This meant contact with the enemy was not imminent. Rollings moved past Morin and whispered to Mckee, giving him the direction of the trail Ayers had discovered. Mckee relaxed and dropped to one knee as he scanned the jungle in front of him.

For the first time since the beginning of the patrol, I felt fatigued. The extra ammo, the steep climb up the mountain, and the one-hundred-degree heat and humidity were beginning to wear me down. The straps from my ammo-laden backpack cut deeply into my shoulders, and my equipment did not feel a part of me. The recon vets like Mckee and Morin moved with ease. They had mastered the load, and I felt that I would do the same, but just then I was enduring the rite of passage without revealing my pain. I fought the temptation of allowing the beauty of the jungle to become a distraction. It was lush and alluring, but I reminded myself that we were on no walk in the park.

My years of football had taught me to ignore pain and to realize that fatigue can cause carelessness, which can lead to injury. "Stay alert," I whispered under my breath as my eyes inspected every inch of jungle in front of me.

Rollings moved up close to me. Through his cupped hands, he began to whisper directly into my ear. "Bill, Sergeant Ayers spotted the enemy moving on a trail two hundred meters below us to the west. It's a big movement, maybe battalion size." Rollings pointed to his map and continued, "Our objective is here, and it looks like this battalion of NVA could be moving through it. We just have to do the grab quickly and quietly because there are so damn many of them." Still pointing to the map, Rollings moved his finger to a circled area, whispering, "This is our extract LZ, in some elephant grass, one hundred meters east of our objective. Can you pack the prisoner that far if we get into the crap? I'll be covering you the whole way." I reassured him with a quick nod. We exchanged quick grins as Rollings gave the signal for the patrol to move out.

Lunch Meat reached the crest of the mountain late in the afternoon. Rollings gave the signal to eat. The team assumed a perimeter and buddied up for chow. One Marine, with barely a sound, opened his C rations while the other Marine stood watch. Sergeant Ayers quietly dug a hole in the soft jungle floor. Each Marine silently passed his empty cans to Ayers, who carefully placed them in the hole and covered it so you did not even know it was there. Force Recon referred to their night quarters in the bush as a harbor site. The narrow ridgeline created a very defendable position for the Marines to spend the night. At last light, the team followed Sergeant Mckee to the highest point of the ridge, where Rollings assigned positions by first pointing to the Marine and then pointing to the ground.

The Marines were close enough to one another to reach over in the night and warn one another of danger or pass the handset for radio watch. Each watch was for one hour, with the handset being passed clockwise after quietly awakening the Marine for his watch. The radio handset was to be placed into the hand of the awakened Marine, never on the ground. Communication was the lifeline of the patrol, and the 1st Force command bunker at An Hoa would be asking Lunch Meat for situation reports all night long. Every Force Recon team member knew that a violation of radio watch procedure would draw a heavy fine when the team returned home.

At last light, each Marine checked his field of fire and sunk his K-bar knife into the ground next to him. The primary radio was positioned in the middle of Lunch Meat's small perimeter. Everyone was to be on full alert the first hour. If the team was going to be hit, it usually happened right after dusk when there was still enough light left to see the Marines' harbor site.

Ayers drew the first watch, and within minutes the 1st Force command bunker was asking for a situation report. Ayers whispered the words "Car lug nut," which meant harbor site secure. Everything was communicated in code words to keep the enemy from understanding the team's reports during a patrol.

I had just dropped off to sleep when I felt someone squeeze my arm. It was Ayers, signaling me to take the handset for my radio watch. Ayers was right in my face. "Sir," he whispered, "are you awake?"

"Yeah," I replied. "I got it."

"It's real quiet out there tonight," Ayers said faintly. His sense of security gave me confidence that the team was truly secure for the night. My watch went by without incident. I passed the radio to Rollings at the end of my watch and fell fast asleep. My first day of patrolling had been relatively uneventful.

At dawn, the jungle began to come alive as though someone was very slowly turning up a song on a radio. Dusk and dawn could be times of great danger for a recon team that was deep in enemy-controlled territory. Lunch Meat had, in the few hours that it had been in the jungle, become a part of the landscape. Now the team had to respect that posture. Yesterday, the sound of the NVA helicopter, their movement up the side of the mountain, and, of course, their presence in such great numbers on the trail had silenced the environment. This was a new day for Lunch Meat, and nature seemed to be at peace with our presence. At first light, only the shadows of the team members were visible, then slowly, the features of each Marine became discernible. Sergeant Mckee looked eager to get moving as he stared intensely into a small reflector mirror and applied green and black camouflage greasepaint to his face. Mckee was a street kid from the Bronx who had grown up learning to live by his wits. To him, Vietnam was just another bad neighborhood. His motto was simply "Do not get caught uninvited in someone else's backyard."

Sergeant Morin rubbed the deep scars on his throat, almost as though he were reminding himself of how dangerous it could be in battle. He stroked his M-60 machine gun with a green cloth as though the weapon were sacred. It was said that four years earlier, when he was struck down by enemy machine-gun fire, the corpsman could not pry Morin's fingers off his M-60. It was not until he passed out and nearly died from lack of blood on the medevac chopper that his weapon could be taken from him.

Sergeant Ayers was nowhere to be seen in the harbor site. A half hour before first light, he had crawled into the jungle to be sure no NVA ambush had been set during the night. Lieutenant Rollings had given Ayers permission to use this tactic, and the rest of the team had been told that Ayers would be outside the harbor site at first light. I surveyed the team members' eyes that first morning in the jungle, trying to read any fear or uneasiness in any of them. Football had taught me a lot about the emotion in men's eyes. The secondary radioman seemed either scared or detached. Rollings was totally comfortable with his command of the patrol. His attitude gave the team confidence.

Rollings leaned over to me and whispered, "I want to be back having a beer in the officers' tent at An Hoa by suppertime." There was something about Rollings's leadership that made war fun. Our friendship had begun back on the airstrip just a few days earlier, but it already felt as if we had known each other much longer. During preparation for the patrol, Rollings treated me like a peer. He was handing me the ball on my first patrol, and I was not about to fumble it. I was going to grab any NVA that I could get my hands on. There was no doubt in my mind that I could get this team a score.

During the first hour of daylight, Lunch Meat sat motionless in the harbor site and listened. If the NVA was looking for us, any premature movement might give the team's position away. Sergeant Ayers quietly appeared at one point in the vigil and then slipped back into the jungle. A few minutes later he surfaced again, this time giving Rollings the thumbs-up. Rollings made a hand-to-mouth motion that signaled the team to go ahead and eat. Once again, the Marines painstakingly opened their C-ration cans and ate in silence. Ayers's chemistry with the team leader really impressed me. He complemented leadership by doing his job thoroughly and professionally. I carefully watched how the team members opened their C rations and put on their greasepaint. When Ayers had finished burying the team's C-ration cans, the team members took turns urinating from a kneeling position facing outboard from the perimeter. Those of the team who had to further relieve themselves moved a few feet into the jungle and did so. Every morning, these rituals were repeated. They followed that order of events religiously before the team leader gave them the signal to move out on patrol. Rollings finally motioned the team to stand. Sergeant Mckee checked the wrist compass that was attached to his black watchband and got a heading. Slowly and cautiously, the team began to head north, down the mountainside.

The terrain began to dictate the team's descent. About midmorning, Sergeant Mckee stopped the team with a clenched fist, then slowly tapped his ear with his left index finger: he had heard something. Sergeant Morin passed the signal to Rollings, and each team member all the way back to Ayers raised a fist and tapped his ear with an index finger. Hand signals were often the lifeline to the patrol. If one team member didn't freeze when he saw the clenched fist meaning "Halt!" the entire patrol could be compromised. Force Recon was no place for the unobservant or undisciplined. Vietnamese voices were often the only early warning that kept a recon team from stumbling into the enemy and blowing any chance of completing the mission.

Mckee surveyed the terrain in front of him, and he was sure of one thing: Lunch Meat would have to move very close to the high-speed trail that the enemy was using if it was to reach the objective by noon. Our exact objective was a spot in some elephant grass along another high-speed trail that ran the length of the valley at the base of the mountain. There were no options but to remain on a northern heading and come dangerously close to what sounded like a large enemy movement. Mckee cautiously moved out with the team in tow. Every Marine was fully aware of the danger ahead. Mckee's movement down the mountain was methodical. Every branch, every vine, every leaf, was carefully pushed back to make room for the patrol. Ayers then carefully replaced everything so that the NVA wouldn't stumble onto the route the team was taking and track it to the objective. Rollings held the team up every few minutes to listen to the voices of the enemy, who were getting dangerously close.

Lunch Meat was moving parallel to the high-speed trail within thirty meters or so of the enemy. Every step was bringing the Marines and NVA that much closer as the terrain funneled the opposing forces to an intersection on the trail just east of where the prisoner grab was to take place. Once again, McKee raised a closed fist. The team froze. We were within ten meters of the well-traveled high-speed trail, and every sound the NVA made seemed to be magnified— the scuffle of their boots, the rattle of their utility gear, their coughs and chatter seemed to be in stereo.

Then a splashing sound filled the air. There must be a stream at the base of the mountain, running parallel to the objective. McKee knew the map didn't show an active stream in that area. Walking in or hanging around a stream was frowned upon by most experienced Force Recon Marines because of the danger of being caught trying to cross it. Streams meant fresh water, and fresh water usually meant NVA would be nearby. Rollings carefully moved past Sergeant Morin and up next to Mckee. After a few seconds, Rollings motioned Mckee to move to the west, away from the trail. Rollings stayed right on Mckee's shoulder, directing him to move toward the stream. Ayers grew especially diligent in restoring the vegetation to its proper place. He covered the Marines' boot tracks by rubbing any prints out with the palm of his hand and then brushing the area with the branch from a bush.

At the edge of the stream, Rollings stopped the patrol. He and Mckee looked left and right like they were at a traffic light. Then, with precision, they stepped into the stream without making a sound. With Rollings's eyes traversing up and down the stream to the left and Mckee covering to the right, they crossed the stream—the water got waist high at one point—and moved into the trees on the other side. After checking out the other side, Rollings signaled Sergeant Morin and the radioman to cross. The team crossed the stream in twos, using the same technique employed by Rollings and Mckee. Ayers walked backward as he crossed, while the secondary radioman and I covered left and right. It took about a half hour for the whole team to cross; all the while the NVA continued to talk aloud and stomp across the stream about fifty meters from our position. Rollings moved the team west, away from the enemy and the water.

Within one hundred meters of the objective, he halted the team and signaled for us to form a perimeter. The perimeter was not as tight as the harbor site because it was a fighting formation. We took up positions equidistant from one another and lay flat on our bellies with weapons to our shoulders. Rollings moved over to me and spoke so softly that it was almost impossible to hear what he was saying. I strained to catch every word as Rollings cupped his hands, put them to his mouth, and spoke directly into my ear, "We are almost there. Remember, it will be Mckee, me, and then you up on the trail. When I say go, jump onto the trail and grab one of them. Mckee and I will have you covered, okay?" I nodded. Then Rollings signaled the team to stand and return to patrol formation. Mckee began to slowly and carefully move the team toward our objective.

My adrenaline began to peak as the team moved into position in the elephant grass next to the high-speed trail. The trail traffic that was moving east was not heavy, which is what Lunch Meat needed for the grab. Most of the NVA troops moving down the mountain must have turned west at the intersection of the two trails. The fact that the main element of the movement would not be moving past Lunch Meat's objective made the grab less complicated.

Mckee, Rollings, and I had barely taken a knee next to the trail when a tough NVA soldier came walking by our position. He was tall and stocky, looking more Chinese than Vietnamese. His olive-green utility shirt seemed new, but his dusty boots looked as if they had plenty of miles on them. Thick muscular calves bulged beneath his thigh-length black pajama shorts, and his AK-47 assault rifle, equipped with a large banana-style ammunition maga-zine, was suspended from a strap across one shoulder. It came to rest on his hip. He had a huge tan pack on his back, with extra grenades and bullets in canvas pouches hanging off a belt around his midsection. This guy, with his high-and-tight haircut, tan face, and cocky expression, looked as if he could kick some serious butt. With no warning that he had spotted us, the NVA soldier passed by Sergeant Mckee, then whirled around, pulling his weapon off his hip. Mckee opened up first, hitting the enemy sol-dier in the legs and dropping him right in his tracks.

"Go, go, go!" Rollings yelled. I quickly jumped onto the trail and grabbed the NVA, stripping him of his AK-47 and slinging it over my own shoulder. Then I pulled the enemy soldier into the elephant grass. Rollings and Mckee provided cover fire so I was able to drag the wounded prisoner about twenty-five meters before encountering a squad of NVA coming through the tall, thick grass toward me. I was compromised and stuck with the prisoner. The enemy squad had moved within ten feet of my position when, from out of nowhere, Rollings appeared and mowed down the squad of NVA with one clip of full-automatic fire from his M-16. A Chicom grenade landed in front of us and the prisoner. The explosion knocked Rollings to the ground, but the prisoner's body shielded me from the shrapnel that zipped through the air. I reached for Rollings's arm and pulled him to his feet. Rollings, with a wound to the forehead, came up off the ground like a wildcat. "Are you okay?" I hollered in Rollings's face. "Damn," Rollings bellowed, reaching for a grenade off his cartridge belt. His eyes were glazed, but he was fighting back.

Lunch Meat's experience was going to have to save this day. The team formed a tight perimeter and killed everything that moved outside it. Sergeant Morin shouted, "Everybody get down, get down, get down!" and Rollings repeated the order. We hit the deck as Morin made a 360-degree sweep of the perimeter with the M-60 machine gun, mowing down the waves of NVA that were about to overrun our position.

"Where the hell did they all come from?" Sergeant Ayers was yelling as he fired a full magazine of M-14 ammunition at the shadowy figures who were firing back while advancing on his position. "I need some help over here," he shouted. Within seconds, Morin was at Ayers's side, pouring rounds out of his M-60. Morin was special: he had a feel for the advance of the enemy. He dropped to one knee and yelled "Cover me" to us. Then he broke open the breech on the M-60 and slapped another belt of ammo into it. He was so quick that we had barely finished another magazine of ammo when he popped back up, laying down a devastating base of fire. Morin's only outward sign of concern was the occasional stroking of the scars on his neck. But he wiped the sweat from his eyes and continued to pour deadly fire on the enemy.

I stayed with the prisoner while the NVA feverishly searched the grass for their comrade. Rollings and Mckee moved between me and the advancing NVA. "Don't let him go, Bill," Rollings said.

"He isn't going anywhere," I shouted back.

Bullets were flying in every direction as the primary radioman yelled to Rollings, "We've got air support on the way." Within minutes, a Huey gunship made its first pass over Lunch Meat's position. Rollings moved off the perimeter and grabbed the handset from his radioman. There was no more whispering. "This is Lunch Meat Six. Who am I talking to?" he barked.

"Ah, Lunch Meat Six, this is Hostage Fluff. How many of you supergrunts are down there? I count seven," the radio receiver squawked. "Seven it is," Rollings returned. "You got a bit of a problem, Lunch Meat. More NVA are moving down the trail and into the grass near your position. I've got fixed-wing coming out to help us, but you best be helping yourselves for now."

"Machine gun over here now, Morin!" Rollings yelled. Morin reported to Rollings's side instantly. "Give me some right *there*," Rollings roared. Morin smiled as he delivered withering fire on the NVA. The blast from Morin's weapon stopped the enemy dead.

Hostage Fluff called to Rollings, "Lunch Meat Six, you okay down there?"

"Roger, Fluff, we're okay," Rollings returned.

"Okay, Lunch Meat, get down. I'm delivering snake and nape to your north near the trail," Fluff said. Without further warning, a Marine Corps Phantom jet screamed low over Lunch Meat's position and dumped napalm within fifty meters of the team's perimeter. Seconds later, as the Marines hugged the ground, another Phantom dropped a load of five-hundred-pound bombs on the NVA who had gotten caught out in the open to the east.

The next message that came over the radio didn't please Rollings at all. "Lunch Meat Six, you need to get back on that trail and move east for two hundred meters so we can get a chopper in to pick you up. That grass you are in is too tall."

"That's been a busy trail all day, Fluff, but we will give it a try," Rollings said. He looked up. "Okay, Lunch Meat, let's move back to the trail. We've got to walk it for two hundred meters to get out of here."

"The prisoner is dead," I shouted back to Rollings.

"What?" Rollings shouted back to me.

"He's dead, damn it, dead!" I repeated.

"Okay, let's get the hell out of here. Just leave him. Morin, you're on point with the M-60. Get us out of here." Morin didn't hesitate; the NVA were temporarily stunned, so it was "now or never." With a battle cry, he cut a path in front of the team right up to the trail. The barrel of his M-60 turned white hot as Morin blasted his way down the trail toward a large NVA reaction force. We all began to yell and scream like crazed men as we fought to break the enemy's hold along the trail. We must have sounded like a 240-man Marine infantry company moving down that trail. Seven Force Recon Marines, with nothing to lose, poured deadly fire in every direction. Unable to hold their positions as Lunch Meat advanced toward its extract LZ, the NVA were diving off both sides of the trail.

Huey and Cobra gun birds fired rockets and machine-gun fire from above while the CH-46 troop transports landed in the tall elephant grass at the edge of the trail. The tailgate of the transport was high above Lunch Meat's reach when we arrived at the extract zone. The crew chief in the 46 waved the team off. The big bird lifted back up and then came down hard on its underbelly, crushing the thick elephant grass beneath it. With the help of the chopper's crew chief, Mckee finally grabbed the tailgate and pulled himself into the bird. Then Sergeant Ayers, acting as a stepladder, allowed other Marines to climb on his back and crawl into the chopper. Finally, Rollings and I reached down and caught hold of Ayers's arms and pulled him on board. Amid a hail of bullets from the intense enemy ground fire, the CH-46 pilot gave the big helicopter full thrust and pulled out of the elephant grass. Within seconds, Lunch Meat was hundreds of feet above the jungle canopy and headed home to An Hoa. The team celebrated their miraculous escape with a long spontaneous series of growls, a Force Recon trademark. The practice was new to me, but I joined in and growled my first "Aruuuuuuura!" I had been through my baptism of fire and earned the right to growl the growl.

When the CH-46 touched down on the airstrip at An Hoa, the chopper's crew chief and pilots removed their headphones and followed the team onto the tarmac. The crew chief grabbed Rollings and excitedly began telling him what the battle looked like from the air. "Man, I counted over fifty NVA laying dead in the elephant grass. At least a hundred were moving on the trail toward your position, and you had another hundred moving down the stream seventy-five meters to your south. We were taking .50-caliber machine-gun fire from a half-dozen positions. God, I don't believe we got you guys out of there."

The pilot looked at me and said, "You guys got a beer around here? I really don't want to fly anymore today; I mean, I've never been in a hotter zone than that." Then, pointing to the tail section of his chopper, he said, "Look at what that .50-caliber fire did to my bird." The tail of the chopper looked like a shredded tin can. The enemy machine-gun fire had left foot-long tears in the metal skin of the craft. Without taking my eyes off the damage to the chopper, I said, "You're right. We owe you a beer. No, hell—we owe you a case of beer." Rollings and the rest of the team and the crew of the chopper broke into laughter.

Two more CH-46 helicopters landed before our ride came to return us to the 1st Force compound. Rick Miller led his team down the rear ramp and onto the tarmac. There was no celebration on the faces of those Marines. Miller was really animated as he walked toward me and Rollings, saying, "Six times I've been shot out, six times today. Look at my jungle cover. I took a round through my jungle cover." Then, pointing back at the chopper as a dead NVA was being carried down the ramp on a stretcher, Miller fumed, "That little s.o.b. almost blew me away in that last LZ. Look, he shot a hole in my jungle cover, damn." The usually calm Miller was obviously rattled by the events of the day.

I knew I needed a couple more snap-in patrols before I would be given my own team. My adrenaline was still pumping, and wanting to be supportive of Miller, I spoke up. "Rick, when are you going back into the bush, buddy?"

"Tomorrow," Miller answered.

"I'd like to run a patrol with you. How about taking me along?"

Miller didn't hesitate. "Sure, Bill, you can run tail-end Charlie because Sergeant Sanders is going on R and R. I need someone to cover the rear of the patrol."

My mouth fell open, and I said, "Tail-end Charlie?"

"Yeah," replied Miller, "tail-end Charlie." I felt the offer from Rick was a real vote of confidence. After all, the guy had four years' experience in Vietnam. At that point, I was glad that I had watched Ayers work for the past couple of days. However, I had questions for Ayers, like where he went when he disappeared from the patrol for up to an hour.

I turned toward Ayers, who had a big smile on his face as he announced to me, "Sir, you're living my dream, because I was getting ready to ask Lieutenant Miller if he would take me." Then Ayers turned to Miller and said, "Well, sir, do you think you could use another man?"

Miller replied, "Who the hell are you?"

"Sgt. Eugene Ayers, sir," Ayers answered quickly.

Miller smiled and said, "Okay, Sgt. Eugene Ayers, we'll see what you got."

I laughed and said, "Let me buy you a beer tonight, Sarge, and we can talk about it. I'll be looking for a good platoon sergeant in a week, and maybe you're him." Ayers replied, "Sir, you are on. I'll see you tonight, and I did hear you say you were buying."

An Hoa had been a beautiful valley before the war. It had been an agricultural center with rich rice crops and beautiful rubber plantations. Alligator Lake wrapped around a luxuriant French resort overlooking the north end of the valley. Some of the wealthiest families of Southeast Asia had once spent their summers vacationing in the famous An Hoa Basin. Now, 1st Force Recon occupied what had once been a prosperous gravel works, just below Alligator Lake. That evening, in the shadow of an old rock crusher, sat Ayers and I. Our broken-down lawn chairs graced the wooden deck at the rear entrance of the officers' tent. A dozen empty beer cans were witness to the several hours we had spent getting to know each other. Ayers was a family-oriented guy. He had never been married, but you could tell talking to him that he loved his sisters, mother, and stepdad. We talked about our homes and families before we got into the finer points of running tail-end Charlie. Neither of us was feeling any pain when Ayers began sharing how he handled bringing up the rear of a recon patrol. His techniques included doglegging, creating false patrol routes, setting ambushes for ·any enemy following the patrol, and much more. "The troops," Ayers said, "always call me Mother because I try to take good care of them. I don't like it, but I know they don't mean any harm. But if I catch one of them calling me Mother, I will kick his butt. Understand." It seemed the nickname had already begun to spread because another sergeant recognized him earlier in the 1st Force mess hall and greeted him at the top of his lungs as "Mother." Ayers and I knew that night that we could work together. Our professional relationship and friendship had begun.

Meanwhile, far from the real war, Defense Secretary Melvin Laird reasoned that if time could be bought to allow U.S. military advisers and instructors to train more South Vietnamese soldiers, the United States could turn the war over to them and leave Vietnam. Laird felt that the only way Nixon could dampen the increasingly wide-spread and vocal criticism of the war was to bring the GIs home rapidly and in quantity. Laird would urge the president to pare the U.S. troop presence from 532,500 to 250,000.

But the president was by no means ready for a unilateral concession of that magnitude. And the president's instincts would prove to be correct. Premature concessions could have totally compromised American troops, especially those units like 1st Force, which were still locked in combat against the North Vietnamese regulars. But neither Nixon nor Laird knew the true magnitude of North

Vietnamese troop strength that was streaming into South Vietnam through entry points in the Central Highlands along the Laotian border. In the spring of 1969, even MACV and the III MAF commanding generals and staff didn't fully comprehend the huge size of the NVA troop transfer as the NVA moved into place for a major summer offensive. The only unit in all of Vietnam that was becoming fully aware that the North Vietnamese Army was up to something big were the ragged recon teams of 1st Force Reconnaissance Company.

CHAPTER 5

Into the Que Sons

Our CH-46 buttonhooked sharply left, then sank suddenly into the open patch of ground below the eighty-foot, layered jungle canopy and quickly disgorged the team, call sign Recline, into the ten-foot elephant grass. We were inserted about a mile south of Landing Zone (LZ) Cutlass on the Yang Brai Ridgeline, just east of the Cai River. The Que Son Mountains were Indian country. Miller had chosen an experienced six-man team. As patrol leader, he was walking deuce point, and as the assistant patrol leader, I would walk tail-end Charlie. Miller and his men had been there a week earlier. No one in the team expected a pleasant reception.

On its last patrol, Recline had confirmed that this remote part of Base Area 112 was infested with units of the 2d North Vietnamese Army Division. The team had observed hundreds of well-equipped, khaki-clad NVA troops on its trails. Intelligence now indicated that Front Four, the headquarters for enemy operations from the Central Highlands to the DMZ, might also be holed up there. Miller was told the brass wanted to know where they were and how well they were equipped. After analyzing the information Recline and other teams retrieved, headquarters would try to puzzle its way through possible enemy capabilities and intentions.

Miller had planned the insert for four in the afternoon to allow Recline just enough time before dark to move sufficient distance from the landing zone to a harbor site. Were they discovered, Miller planned to use the cover of darkness to evade North Vietnamese Army patrols in pursuit.

Although it was already approaching late afternoon, the heat and humidity that encased the thick secondary growth under the jungle ceiling was stifling. Two relatively new members of Recline, lance corporals Rush and Reed, on their third patrols, were especially wary as the team leaped from the tail ramp of the 46, then froze, listening for sounds of enemy presence after the chopper swiftly climbed out of the zone.

Knowing that the NVA had to have heard, and might even have seen, the helicopter land, Miller hand-signaled the point man, Corporal Taylor, the direction of movement and hurried the team through the thick grass toward the tree line. Miller disliked the team's vulnerability during inserts and extracts: he equated it to a jet pilot's "controlled crash" on each recovery aboard an aircraft carrier.

We were already sweating profusely in spite of having flown at high altitude during the twenty-minute trip from the company base camp in An Hoa. My adrenaline was high, as it always would be at the start of a patrol, and my heart pounded rapidly, seeming to reverberate from my head down. Thank God the LZ wasn't hot, I mused. Got to find some cover and move quickly, gain some distance from this damn LZ.

Sergeant Ayers was positioned near the middle of the team, between the two radio operators, so he could back up the patrol leader in monitoring all transmissions. Ayers had done most of his patrolling with the grunts during his first tour. He told me he had been wounded once when he was a rifle squad leader in 1966. Ayers had been in his

share of firefights. When Rush stumbled under the weight
of his combat load, Ayers grabbed his web gear and
yanked him to his feet as the team sought the protection of
the heavy growth on the periphery of the zone.

At the tree line, Miller gestured the recon Marines into a
hasty perimeter. Providing security in the patrol's rear, I
backpedaled the way I had seen Ayers do it so I could close
with the rest of Recline. Suddenly my ankle turned under
me as I fell back into a small one-man spider hole dug
by the NVA. Regaining my balance, I saw that the LZ
and surrounding ground was a matrix of foxholes, slit
trenches, and spider holes. The platoon-size NVA fortifi-
cation was thinly camouflaged but clearly would have
made the LZ an indefensible killing zone had the NVA
been home when the team arrived. Boot prints in fresh dirt
and paths through the dense grass signaled recent NVA
presence.

Realizing the enemy's proximity, I hustled to rejoin Recline in the scrub cover under the canopy. As soon as
I reached the team, Miller, raising a clenched fist, motioned all to freeze. Less than five yards away through the
bushes and trees, we watched as a squad of enemy soldiers
double-timed down a trail leading to the landing zone.
Dressed in khakis and wearing pith helmets, each NVA
soldier was armed with an AK-47 assault rifle. Seconds
later, another fifteen marched rapidly by as we crouched
motionless, our patterned camouflage utilities blending in
with the lush foliage.

Miller and I realized that by sheer luck we had caught
the NVA off guard. There'd been no sentries posted in or
near the LZ. The pungent odor of *nuoc mam*—a fermented
fish sauce used by the Vietnamese to season their otherwise bland daily ration of rice—told the Marines of Recline that our insert timing had been perfect: just before

the bird hit the zone and spit out the team, the enemy
had withdrawn from the zone and were squatting over an
early-evening meal around platoon cook fires concealed
under the jungle canopy. Hearing the CH-46, the NVA had
rushed up the hill to investigate. Recline's well-practiced
speed exiting the insert bird and clearing a landing zone
may have saved the day. At least for the moment. The
trails that Uncle Ho's foot soldiers had beaten around their
trench works obscured the path Recline created as we
quickly sought the jungle cover.

Miller, still fearing detection, motioned me to backtrack
to conceal the patrol's presence by straightening the grass
we had trampled as the team rushed to the protection of
the brush at the clearing's edge. I crawled back into the
zone and began to cover the trail by bending the elephant
grass back into the vertical. Knowing the NVA were near, I
thought the task a stupid risk, but as Miller's assistant patrol leader, I followed the order. Since it was only my
second patrol, I overrode my own instincts.

Suddenly, two NVA soldiers were standing over me,
talking rapidly, not more than five feet away. In spite of
their relative youth, they looked like seasoned soldiers.
Their weapons, web gear, and battle equipment were
serviceable and worn confidently and professionally. A
sparse screen of tall grass was all that separated me from
them. I was on my back, holding my breath, M-16 selector
switch on full automatic. I partially depressed the trigger.
My pulse thundered so loud I feared they might hear
me. My painted face was now awash in sweat. One more
step, I thought, and I'll blow your heads off. The ten seconds they stood near me seemed an eternity. Without
warning the two soldiers walked off in the opposite direction, leaving me gasping for breath.

I raised my head to peek at the open area and saw a

platoon of perhaps thirty NVA soldiers methodically combing the field. Unwilling to chance compromise, I slithered backward quickly to join Recline in the relative concealment of the jungle, carefully lifting the grass behind me back into its vertical position as I moved.

When I returned, Miller was trying to reach company headquarters to provide a situation report and to tell them he feared Recline had landed dead in the center of a large enemy unit, actual size unknown. Unable to get communications with the company combat operations center (COC) in An Hoa, he then called a platoon-size radio-relay site set up on a ridgeline three miles away. "Haven, Haven," Miller whispered, "this is Recline. Can you read me? Over." We had been on the ground less than a half hour, but the mental fatigue was already beginning to show, particularly among the two junior patrol members. We huddled in a tight security perimeter, facing outward, sensing we were in trouble even though, as yet, we were undetected. All knew they were in the midst of a large enemy encampment. The question was how large and how could Recline escape. Miller and I hoped the NVA would conclude our helicopter had made a "false insert," a tactic frequently used by the Marines to deceive the enemy of the actual insert location of recon teams. Ayers feared the NVA's counterreconnaissance teams might already be on our tails.

As the NVA steadily searched the ground, Miller persistently tried to reach either the radio-relay site or Home Plate, the recon company headquarters some fifteen miles away. As was often the case, he couldn't connect on the radio, so we were left in the breach with no other support than what was organic to the patrol. Miller knew the weak internal firepower of the six-man team would be fatally inadequate if we were detected and had to fight without air or artillery support. Recline could only defend itself for a short time without supporting arms. If the team made contact, Miller feared we wouldn't survive long enough to be extracted.

Ten minutes later, Recline was finally contacted by High Flyer, a twin-engine OV-10 spotter plane operated by a pilot and an aerial observer trained to call for and adjust supporting arms. The plane also served as an almost foolproof radio-relay platform, able to maintain near continuous line-of-sight contact with the team. When communications were lost following our insert, the recon company headquarters tasked the OV-10 to locate and determine the situation of the patrol. The aircraft was at about five thousand feet and, given the frequent presence of Marine air assets, attracted little attention from the NVA.

"High Flyer, this is Recline. We are surrounded, may need an emergency extract," Miller whispered into the radio handset.

"Can you clear the zone so we can get you out?" High Flyer asked.

Miller rolled his eyes at me, then replied quickly, "We can't hold this zone without a lot of casualties. If we get detected before nightfall, we may be dead anyway. For now, just tell Haven we're already in trouble, over."

"Sit tight," High Flyer said, "we'll stay close. If you make contact, run for the LZ. We'll prep it, call an emergency extract bird, and do everything we can to get you out."

Miller rolled his eyes again and shook his head at me, disgusted with the air winger's inability to grasp the situation on the ground. "If you prep the LZ, the NVA will join us in the damn tree line and find us for sure," Miller said.

"For now, High Flyer, just keep contact with us while we try to work a miracle and find some safe ground."

Listening to Miller, I recalled that he had been begging headquarters to find more LZs or make them because the NVA had all existing LZs in the rugged terrain mapped and monitored. Sergeant Ayers, who was also listening to Miller, was beginning to feel queasy but wasn't sure if it was from fear or from the sickening smell of *nuoc mam* that hung heavily in the dense air under the canopy. When darkness fell, we crept silently deeper into the jungle, avoiding trails, while seeking more cover and higher ground. As we ascended, the night campfires of the NVA soldiers below us were barely visible through the layered foliage. With darkness, the team's confidence grew. I had seen quickly in my previous snap-in patrol that the night was always a reconnaissance patrol's ally.

Taylor, who'd been Miller's point man for six months, led the team into a harbor site in heavy brush, tucked well back off what appeared to be a major trail. Miller signaled the team to set up the night's watch. Far too frequently, it seemed, enemy soldiers in small groups moved up and down the trail that wound up being only forty feet away. In spite of our hunger, Miller wouldn't allow us to open C-ration cans for fear the noise would cause detection. My stomach growled so loudly, I thought enemy trail walkers would hear it, but I had no desire to risk opening a can. A full stomach could wait.

At 9:00 P.M., the recon patrol had already been on the ground five hours. Other than for Miller's sporadic radio transmissions, hardly a word had been whispered among us. The sign language and intuition of a well-trained patrol, as well as fear of compromise, negated the need to talk. A 50 percent alert was established. In spite of the enemy's nearness, the Marines not on watch quickly

drifted into uneven sleep. In my short time in country,
I had begun to marvel at my ability to divorce myself
from my fears or, at least, to control them, even in life-
threatening predicaments. Mosquitoes were plentiful in
the damp jungle undergrowth, but the physical and mental
fatigue still permitted us at least restless sleep. At midnight, when he was sure our position was safe, Miller told
High Flyer, who'd already refueled twice and returned, to
go home but to check back in at first light. NVA activity
along the ridgeline would increase at that time.

Under the tiered hood of the jungle, darkness slowly
turned to dawn. The eerie mountainous refuge, backyard
to the NVA, slowly returned to life. Birds called. A light
breeze swept through the patrol's harbor site. A rifle shot,
above us on the ridgeline, shattered the deceptive peace
of daybreak, and the Marines of Recline, suddenly fully
awake, were again alerted to its perilous situation.

Team members, thinking as one, began to replenish the
camouflage paint on their faces and exposed skin. Most
had sweated off the bulk of the previous day's camouflage.
Another shot was fired, and Rush and Reed flinched re-
flexively. Miller and I, realizing NVA trail monitors were
signaling to units camped in the remote mountains, whispered assurances to the team. Nothing to fear. Our position
was still safe. We had not been detected.

With the growing light, the NVA began again to shuttle up
and down the trail, individually and in small groups or units.
Miller and Taylor crawled within fifteen feet of the jungle
path, still in very thick vegetation but close enough to observe enemy movement. In half an hour, Miller recorded in
his patrol book over one hundred NVA soldiers, many very
well armed and equipped.

The enemy moved with a loose, assured confidence, as
though they owned the ground. They were unaware of our

eyes. Should the team accept the risk, we could rain artillery and air strikes on the NVA units once their precise locations were fixed. But at that point, we were focused on survival. Miller had decided that fire support would be called only to cover the extract.

As Miller and Taylor monitored the movement on the trail, we heard the enemy crossing the creek in a deep draw below them. We also heard hammering and what sounded like digging on the hill behind us. The smell of cooking food wafted through the jungle on a faint breeze. For Miller and me, all that NVA activity confirmed our fears about how tenuous our situation was. During the morning hours, hundreds of NVA soldiers, almost in spitting distance of the team, continued to travel along the ridge. When movement along the ridgeline lessened, an enemy trail monitor seemed always in the vicinity just above us, laughing and joking with the passing troops. Occasionally, when no one was around, the sentry would lean his weapon against a tree or bush and sing Vietnamese songs.

When there was enough background noise and activity in the encampment, Miller would radio higher headquarters and chastise them for the team's predicament. The radio relay told Recline the company would get them out at first opportunity. Miller had decided that after we were extracted, he would destroy the NVA encampment with air strikes and artillery concentrations. In the meantime, the recon team was trapped, hemmed in by enemy activity on all sides. Miller shook his head and smiled cynically at me when the radio-relay site told him that headquarters wanted them to sit tight at least for another night. For the rest of the day we lay low, remaining as motionless as our weary bodies allowed. Sleep that night was even more troubled than on the first.

The following morning, Recline was again startled by the dawn signal shots. Troop movements were renewed, but the pace had slowed to about fifty soldiers passing each hour. Miller dutifully kept score in his patrol book. After recording his three hundredth sighting, he turned to me, raised his eyebrows, and smiled. "We're never gonna get out of here," he mouthed to me, not wanting the other team members to hear him.

We heard a sudden clatter on the trail. Miller and I thought we had been detected. The team quickly realized, however, from what sounded like good-natured banter, that they needn't fear for the moment. The NVA seemed to be laughing. Miller and Taylor crept closer to the high-speed mountain trail and recognized the cause of the enemy's joviality. Two soldiers held between them a squealing pig that had been hog-tied to a bamboo pole. Some of the NVA soldiers were going to have a rare banquet that night. During the commotion on the trail above us, Ayers seized the opportunity to move around a bit and stretch his stiff, weary body. Rush and Reed—who'd developed colds during the first forty-eight hours of the patrol—buried their faces in their poncho liners and rasped and coughed to clear the phlegm from their throats.

The tedious confinement of our lair was taking its toll physically and psychologically. Muscles ached from countless hours of sitting fear-struck and motionless. We were afraid that any movement might cause discovery. For two days, no one had eaten. The men rolled over to relieve themselves just inches from where they lay. We slept, at best, sporadically and restlessly. We also realized that we were beginning to stink. Flies had become a greater nuisance. Ants and mosquitoes seemed hungrier.

The radio watch was again set up as Recline began its third night in its bamboo prison. Haven, the radio-relay site, passed Recline's traffic to headquarters in An Hoa. Miller, ever the cynic, was convinced the brass didn't believe the NVA troop concentrations we had reported. He suspected the III MAF command figured Recline was inflating numbers of enemy sightings to compel an early extract. Miller and I were convinced by then that the team had been planted in the middle of a regimental base camp.

Our predicament inspired the full range of emotions from abject fear to death-wish exhilaration. Recline had definitely been living on the edge for the last seventy-two hours. That night, Miller and I considered all our alternatives for escape. In only one direction, across the main trail to the east, did it appear there was little or no activity. That would be our initial route out. The team would cross the trail at night, but we would not begin our escape until first light, when NVA traffic on trails and in the camps would mask the sound of the team's movement through the heavy brush. Before Recline attempted to withdraw to the extract LZ, Miller would call close air support on station, ensuring it was ready to respond immediately. Miller and I also preplanned artillery concentrations with designated target numbers to cut response time. During the night, the two artillery batteries dedicated to support us preset the target firing data.

When dawn approached and we decided to cross the trail into the preliminary position for withdrawal, Miller discovered that the avenue we believed to be clear was occupied. The NVA were in fact constructing what appeared to be a shelter or storage site, and our route would take us directly through enemy positions. We would have to sit tight yet another day and devise an alternate plan.

The Marines of Recline still hadn't eaten as we began our fourth day on the Yang Brai Ridgeline. By then, our water supply was perilously low. In spite of limited movement, we had all sweated steadily, and our bodies begged for more water than the five canteens each of us had carried and consumed. The stream in the deep draw behind us was accessible, but during the day especially, far too much enemy activity in that area prevented our risking a water run.

At around 9:00 A.M., we heard a commotion and animated chatter about fifty yards along the trail to the southwest. The trail monitor, about forty feet above us, began shouting excitedly to other soldiers in the area. Shortly, Miller and I and the rest of the team could hear female voices. Miller and Taylor again crawled close enough to the jungle path to see fourteen Vietnamese women, all very young and beautiful, walk by the trail monitor, who was now catcalling at them enthusiastically. Farther down the trail, the women must have taken a path to the stream in the draw behind us because, for the next hour, we could hear them frolicking in the water below. The presence of women fueled our belief that the team had discovered a major enemy encampment.

In spite of sporadic flashes of adrenaline caused by occasional movement on the trail, the hours crawled by with agonizing slowness. Late in the afternoon, a light rain began. Soon it became an unusual premonsoon downpour. For the Marines of Recline, rain had never felt so good.

Knowing the heavy downpour would drive the NVA to shelter, at Miller's direction we took the opportunity to get up on our knees, move about cautiously, and wipe off the accumulated tropical grime. With a rare background of thunder and lightning, the rain cascaded through the myriad openings in the canopy, and the jungle reverberated with the rush of countless little waterfalls. I quickly inhaled a can of beef and potatoes and followed that with a second ration, pork and beans. My counterparts did likewise, eating ravenously. Using ponchos to collect the rainwater, in short order we refilled our canteens and guzzled the precious liquid till we were completely satisfied. After wolfing our C rats, we cleaned the food cans and stuffed them into our packs, careful not to leave any obvious traces of our presence. Miller strictly adhered to the company standard operating procedure on maintaining stealth.

Movement in the jungle had ceased during the downpour. Even the bothersome trail monitor had disappeared into shelter. After about half an hour, the deluge became a drizzle. The pause had given the team the chance to towel off, ventilate clogged body pores, and cool down. We all felt more alert, as if we had been born again. Even so, I jumped when I heard an unusual click. I spun around to face Miller, who grinned broadly and handed me a warm can of Budweiser. Miller, the company maverick, fought the war on his own terms. The team passed the can around, each taking a healthy pull. Then, rejuvenated, we refocused on the mission and our continuing dilemma.

After a while, the rain had slackened off, but the layers of jungle foliage dripped for hours. We resumed our strict security posture in the dense scrub growth. The six of us sat in a tight circle, weapons positioned, grenades at the ready, facing outward once again. Miller ran a radio check with the relay site to make sure our lifeline to support was intact. It was.

Now reenergized, I turned my attention again to the team's unchanged predicament. My mind raced as I considered the dilemma. What do we do if detected? Which direction do we run? How do we break contact and then get out through this canopy if we can't find open ground? If we get hit hard, given the density of the NVA along the ridgeline, will we get out at all? Will another patrol find our bodies? I remembered also that, in two days, I had hoped to be drinking a beer in the company headquarters at An Hoa and celebrating my twenty-fourth birthday. Just then, living to do that seemed the ultimate goal.

As the weather tempered, the enemy came back to life. Movement and talking could be heard along the ridge to the southwest. Smoking a cigarette, the trail monitor resumed his watch. In the distance, the sounds of soldiers at work cutting, hammering, and digging picked up. Miller and I, listening intently to our adversaries, looked at one another and shook our heads; we were both wondering if it would ever be possible to escape. With our senses heightened by the four-day ordeal, every noise and movement sent a shiver up our spines.

Miller began to aggressively press headquarters for an emergency extract. He was convinced after four days, hunkered down in an NVA encampment that seemed permanent, that every hour we remained increased the risk of the team's destruction. "Haven, Haven, this is Recline," Miller whispered, "it's time to get us out."

Haven replied, "Roger, Recline, extract is scheduled for first light tomorrow. Send us your plan." In hushed conversation, Miller and I devised two options. One called for extract through the jungle canopy on a cable ladder that could be lowered, if necessary, from 125 feet above the ground. The other, if we could safely get to open ground, would be a normal helicopter landing zone extract. The ladder was preferred because it was quicker and didn't require the chopper to hover, exposing the team or the chopper to ground fire while we were on the ladder. With NVA concentrated all around us, Miller and I planned for a withdrawal under pressure. Knowing that the ladder was a safer bet, Miller requested it. Artillery on-call fires were plotted along the route, beginning with the position we then occupied and extending to our anticipated extract point, about thirteen hundred yards to the northeast. Before moving out, Miller would call Haven to make sure all our support was ready, the dedicated artillery battery, the OV-10 spotter plane, and all the fixed-wing aircraft support headquarters could muster. Miller expected mayhem on the extract. All these assets had to be ready at 0530.

Miller and I spent the next two hours outlining contingency plans. We next briefed the team in sign language and whispers before setting the watch and bedding down for the night. We were all pumped up at the prospect of extract and escape. The team would cross the trail and move north by northeast at about a sixty-degree azimuth. If we could avoid contact, at least serious contact, moving in that direction, map study indicated we'd hit a creek and then some open ground after about three quarters of a mile.

At 0430, five days and four nights after being dumped into an NVA stronghold, Recline held a silent reveille and prepared to escape. If it became a shoot-out, the odds were not in our favor, even with our advantages in air and artillery support.

Miller assumed his position as deuce point behind Taylor, the point man. Having been deep in NVA country many times before with Taylor, in "deep crap" a few times, Miller had confidence in Taylor's instincts and tactical abilities. Once again, I assumed tail-end Charlie security, my eyes wide, senses peaked. I was ready. Sergeant Ayers positioned himself between the two radio operators, Rush and Reed, and winked at the young Marines in an attempt to ease their tension. We were all scared, but for the experienced patrol members, it was a controlled fear. They knew that if we executed the plan right, we would get out of our fix and put another big hurt on Charlie. All of us were on our feet, ready to break brush as quietly as was humanly possible.

Miller snapped his fingers and gestured to the team, now standing belly to butt, to take a three-minute security halt before moving out. Miller wanted to let the blood flow fully back into our legs and to listen and look for any sign of the enemy before stepping out onto the trail.

After sitting and lying in the same position for over four days, like the rest of Recline, I struggled at first to regain my equilibrium. I stood in place and quietly shook each leg and arm and methodically flexed my fingers and hands into fists, and then opened and closed them again repeatedly as we waited. It was a technique I had developed as a football player: it helped me relax and focus. My adrenaline was high. It was game time!

As the point man took his first, not entirely silent, step on the damp jungle earth, I realized that the team had developed a false sense of security during our four-day stay on the Yang Brai Ridgeline. I saw us as an awkward newborn insect emerging from a cocoon, for the first time fully vulnerable to the outside world. With a renewed realization of our precarious position, I suddenly felt ponderous and weak. We were all exhausted, physically and emotionally. Time, I thought, to tighten up the execution of the patrol; the team could not afford any mistakes if we hoped to survive.

Having observed the trail monitor for four nights, we knew he either moved his location from about midnight to dawn or that he slept along the trail. We also knew activity along the ridgeline didn't begin until just after first light, about 0600, so we would have about an hour and fifteen minutes of darkness to clear the NVA encampment. As the team slowly crept out of the dense foliage, we quickly discovered not a single jungle path, but two trails wide enough to drive trucks on. From where the stars were visible through the layers of overhead cover, it appeared that the trails were laid out under the canopy so they couldn't be seen from the air. The ridgeline was much more open than we had realized. The brush had been cut and trimmed to make the trails fully trafficable, even for wheeled vehicles. Rest areas for troops on the hoof were carved into the jungle cover, and water was staged in makeshift buckets.

During this most quiet time of night, roughly an hour and a half before dawn, Recline had to clear the area. In pairs, one Marine looking each way, we stealthily moved northeast across the trail, using the vegetation for concealment where we could. The team inched along cautiously, deliberately, padding the dew-covered ground softly. To Miller's surprise, about five hundred yards along our selected route, the team walked into a deep bomb crater that afforded a wide circular opening through the double canopy, easily large enough to hover a helicopter and drop the cable ladder. The undergrowth around the crater also provided some concealment. By then we had been on the move for about forty-five minutes.

It was a half hour before morning twilight. Miller decided to take a risk, even though we hadn't fully cleared the NVA camp. I felt my blood surge in my chest as I peered from the crater into the open sky. The one thing we all quickly recognized was that we had an opening, an extract point, even if the bird couldn't sit down. We also had concealment, and our firepower was poised to strike. Most significant, for the moment at least, we still had the element of surprise.

After waiting another fifteen minutes, Miller called for the extract. "Haven, this is Recline," Miller said. "We're ready to come out. Give me all the fixed-wing and artillery you can, on my command, when the extract bird's inbound."

"Roger, Recline, standing by," Haven replied. "High Flyer will be on station in ten minutes to adjust fires."

Ayers huddled over Reed, the second radio operator, intently monitoring Miller's transmissions. I provided security on the downhill side of the crater. With artillery and close air support to suppress NVA reaction, Miller called for a CH-46 helicopter cable ladder extract through the near ninety-foot canopy. The crater was about two hundred meters down the slope from the top of the ridgeline, with what seemed about one hundred meters of dense jungle cover around it. Miller's plan was to bracket the crater with supporting fires, close air support—snake and napalm ("snake and nape")—along the ridgeline and artillery fires on the downward side of the slope. His hope was to mask the sound, and location, of the extract bird amid all the destruction being delivered by supporting arms. He was playing the odds, hoping the team could remain undetected, at least until the cable was dropped into the three-foot grass at the heart of the crater.

Only one CH-46 would be needed to extract the team, but headquarters would send a section of two, in case one bird became a casualty. The transports would be escorted by a pair of Cobra gunships, whose crews would be prepared with rockets and miniguns to isolate the zone or suppress enemy fire and maneuver tactics.

At nearly 5:30 A.M., Recline was a little more than thirty minutes away from extract. Feelings of anticipation virtually pulsed in us. Miller made contact with the OV-10 and gave his position. As Miller had requested, it was the same OV-10 crew he'd been working with since the insert. So there was no confusion about Recline's location. Miller explained that after crossing the ridge trail, Recline had stayed in the jungle foliage contouring the high ground moving to the northeast. "High Flyer, this is Recline.

We're now at Grid 845232, in a bomb crater about one hundred feet wide."

High Flyer acknowledged, "Roger, Recline, you're about half a mile east of where you've been the last four days. In fifteen minutes, when I have a little more light, I'll locate your position easily. It's gonna be a beautiful morning."

"Roger, High Flyer, the timing's critical. There are bad guys all around us. When the extract bird is inbound, you gotta rip the ridgeline up to keep their heads down while we extract."

The team set up a perimeter around the crater, waiting for dawn. The patrol leader's plan was to strike hard at first light, just early enough for the extract bird to identify the zone, but before the NVA encampment fully came to life. Miller knew the team's chances were best if he nailed the enemy before reveille was complete, before the base camp was fully alive, armed, and alert.

At 0545, about fifteen minutes before the trail monitors normally fired their signal shots up and down the ridgeline, the extract bird, call sign Mailman, escorted by Cobra gunships, reported inbound, five minutes out. High Flyer, three thousand feet above, had identified the zone and had a section of F-4 Phantoms on station with snake and nape ready to strike. On Miller's command, two 155mm artillery batteries would lay a rectangular blanket of steel two hundred yards downslope of the crater to cut off NVA movement from the draw below. Miller was ready to pull the trigger.

Suddenly, a trail monitor fired the first signal shot on the ridgeline above them. Quickly two more shots echoed responses from either flank. The NVA were holding reveille.

"High Flyer, this is Recline, bring in the snake and nape

on top of the ridgeline, Grid 842235. Extract bird inbound, four minutes out."

"Roger, Recline, I'll blow the ridge. Stand by to mark your position with smoke if we get too close. Keep your heads down, we're comin' in."

A minute later, the OV-10 dove toward the ridge, drilling two white-smoke rockets almost dead center on the trail above to mark for the Phantoms. The team immediately heard orders being shouted as the encampment sprang to life. Thirty seconds later, the Phantoms screamed over the target at treetop level and hurled their first load of bombs. An incredible yellow-red flash lit a two-hundred-meter stretch of ridgeline, and a thundering concussion shook the hill mass and reverberated through the surrounding mountains. The first pass was a package of 250-pound bombs. Napalm would follow.

"Recline, this is Mailman. We're inbound, two minutes out."

"Roger, Mailman, ready to mark zone with smoke," Miller said calmly, trying not to betray his emotions to the new guys, Rush and Reed. Now that Miller was excited, the crazy—yet poised and professional—side of him was taking over. All his fears were gone: it was time to execute the plan.

Like the rest of the patrol, I felt a powerful energy that seemed to course swiftly along my spine as the shock of the explosions above heaved the earth and jungle around us. For the first time in four days, my confidence grew. I turned to Rush, who would precede me and Miller onto the ladder, and told him to stay alert and get ready. As the OV-10 spotter plane swooped in to mark the target for a second strike, the Marines of Recline heard the heavy rattle of the enemy's .50-caliber antiaircraft machine guns. By that time, the ridgeline was wild with activity, and Miller feared the NVA were moving off the ridge for cover on the slopes.

Miller called the extract birds urgently, "Mailman, this is Recline, keep comin'. You need to get us out now."

"Roger, Recline, we've got air strikes in sight, two klicks in front of us. Mark your zone." Miller popped a yellow smoke in the middle of the crater and watched as it curled upward through the opening in the canopy toward the pale morning sky.

Mailman responded. "I have your yellow smoke, Recline. I'll be over the zone in thirty seconds. Take cover. The Cobras are comin' in to neutralize the zone."

Miller immediately called for the artillery targets plotted below them on the slope, as much to distract and confuse as to ward the enemy off. The F-4s made a second pass, and five hundred yards of hilltop exploded again, that time with the brilliant and merciless yellow, white, and purple flashes of napalm, which from the air seemed to engulf the entire top of the ridge. Just then three NVA, running for safety from the hell above, blundered through the brush toward the crater, not yet seeing Recline. Blind to our position in the crater, they ran right by us without firing a shot.

As Mailman was in his final approach, the Cobra gunships were engaging targets on the periphery of the zone. Now the extract bird was hovering about one hundred feet above the team, and the ladder was dropped, the bottom rungs snaking about the weeds in the crater, as the pilot struggled to hold a steady hover. Miller, who had previously told Mailman the zone was clear, now shouted into the handset, "The zone is hot. Bring the gunships in closer and get us out, now!"

As the incoming fire intensified around the crater, the steady *whumpf* of artillery explosions below us added to the bedlam. The yelling and shouted commands throughout the jungle told us the NVA camp was in chaos. Miller immediately called for another fire-for-effect from the artillery batteries, this time walking the rounds in one hundred yards closer to our position.

With the ladder now in the crater, the team was executing the extract drill. Taylor got on the ladder first. Fastening himself with a safety rope and snap link, he was quickly followed by Rush and Reed and Ayers, who checked to ensure the ropes were secured to the ladder. Heavy fire was pouring into the crater from the uphill side, and we returned fire frantically.

Finally, the Cobras screamed in and pulled into a sixty-degree nose-down hover on two sides of the crater and began to saturate the heavy jungle on its edges with minigun fire. Given all the enemy activity, Miller and I understood that the extract was our first and last chance. The heavy thud of the Cobras' 2.75-inch rockets was followed by the whine of shrapnel, which cut vicious swaths of foliage, then streaked through the air around the crater.

Despite the suppressive fire, the extract choppers and gunships were now taking steady hits from ground fire. Ayers snapped himself onto the ladder, then fired several bursts at the muzzle flashes around the crater. Miller looked at me and yelled above the din of battle, "Let's get the hell outta here!"

The gunships circled the crater, concentrating their fires on the enemy hidden in the jungle, momentarily neutralizing it. Miller and I leaped onto the cable ladder. Before we could snap on, the crew chief, watching the firefight from the transport's tail ramp, signaled the pilots to extract. The 46 pulled vertically out of the zone until the one-hundred-foot ladder was above the treetops. Then the pilot dropped the transport's nose and accelerated down the slope toward the valley before finally beginning a rapid ascent. The ladder, with us all attached, extended diagonally from the line of flight and looked like the tail of a giant kite. As Mailman cleared the zone, the gunships fired their last volleys and peeled off in trace of the 46s, taking position on the flanks of the transports as they gained altitude.

Miller smiled at me. "We made it, Bill," he yelled. "Thank God, we made it!" Soaring above the Que Sons at about five thousand feet, the team enjoyed the rush of the wind and the sweet solace of escape. As Mailman and its escorts followed the Thu Bon River toward An Hoa Combat Base, the Phantoms unloaded their final bag of bombs, another mixture of snake and nape, and the ridgeline erupted brutally one last time. Within minutes after all aircraft cleared the airspace above the NVA base camp, a B-52 bomber, flying above the clouds, opened its bomb bay doors and unloaded tons of munitions on the base camp, sending shock waves for miles in every direction.

While Recline was heading back to An Hoa, still suspended on the cable ladder beneath the CH-46, Rollings's team, Lunch Meat, was going into action. They were being inserted into a hot zone about a mile west of the Yang Brai Ridgeline. Their mission was to assess the damage that the B-52 Arc Light had inflicted on the base camp. Rollings's team did not even get on the ground, despite the devastating power of the million-dollar B-52 air strike. Nine .50-caliber machine-gun positions opened up on Rollings's chopper, almost blowing it out of the sky when one of the rounds struck a rotor blade.

The remaining 1st Force lieutenants, Champe, Lowder, Hansen, and Ritchie, were glued to the radio in the command bunker, monitoring Recline's extract from and Lunch Meat's insert into the enemy base camp. The lieutenants let out a growl when word came that Recline and Lunch Meat were both safely headed back to An Hoa. Major Simmons really got fired up during Rollings's aborted insert when he heard the aerial observer counting and reporting the positions of *nine* .50-caliber machine guns. Simmons slammed his fist down on his desk and pointed to Captain Williams, saying, "Get Miller in here as soon as he lands. The division G-2 and III MAF intelligence will want to debrief him up at headquarters in Da Nang. We're putting a team back in that base camp area to find out who the hell these bad guys are. We should know that area like the back of our hand by now. Get a team ready to go back in just as quickly as we can."

Showing no emotion, Captain Williams simply replied, "Yes, sir." The lieutenants stood silent, knowing full well that the NVA would obviously enjoy making an example of a 1st Force Recon team. The lieutenants were also having doubts about how much confidence the major really had in them as team leaders. They had witnessed the attitude in the command bunker while Miller and I were stuck in the base camp. The word in the rear was that, at first, the brass didn't believe Recline's reports. It wasn't until a friend of Miller's at division weighed in on behalf of Rick that the reports were taken seriously. All the lieutenants were aware that their integrity was being questioned. Running the patrols into those enemy-infested areas was one thing, but not being believed or being second-guessed by the admin people was more than the lieutenants could bear.

Recline's and Lunch Meat's safe arrival back to the 1st Force Recon Compound sparked a victory party among the lieutenants. I began to celebrate my twenty-fourth birthday with a warm beer and some damp potato chips. I had never valued my birthday the way I did that particular one, on April 18, 1969. Most of the preceding five days, I had spent wondering if I would live to see it. I counted it a miracle, and my father's admonition and the chaplain's final word to me at Quantico were fresh in my mind. In spite of the poor odds of surviving my first two patrols, I felt that somehow my time in Vietnam was being divinely orchestrated. I had decided, while lying in that enemy base camp for four days, that if I made it out, it was because God was looking out for me.

A few days after Recline's miraculous escape from the enemy base camp, back in Washington, D.C., Secretary of Defense Laird was about to make an announcement that would further imperil the lives of the men of 1st Force. He took a White House elevator down to the pressroom, where dozens of reporters had gathered. The room was very quiet as the audience waited for Laird to step to the microphone. The room exploded with questions after Laird announced, "The United States will begin to Vietnamize the war by handing it over to the South Vietnamese Army. The president and I caution the American people that it would not be wise to discuss troop withdrawals while the enemy is conducting an offensive. Although major battles seem to have ceased," he continued, "our small units are reporting increased infiltration into the rural areas of South Vietnam."

It was clear to the world that in spite of the huge buildup of NVA soldiers, the Nixon administration wanted to distance itself from what had been perceived as President Johnson's war. The administration was secretly beginning to lay the groundwork for the United States' withdrawal from South Vietnam. No one was fooled by Laird's announcement, especially the North Vietnamese. Nixon, not wanting to be caught in the same mire as his predecessor, had already set the withdrawal up in his inauguration speech in January, when he stated that "after a period of confrontation, we are entering an era of negotiation." The Gallup polls showed that 42 percent of the American public favored a withdrawal, one that would move quickly. First Force's mission was about to get tougher than ever.

CHAPTER 6

The Covenant

Prior to the arrival of the new crop of lieutenants to 1st Force in early 1969, Major Roger Simmons had labored under extreme adverse conditions. His first few months as company commander in late 1968 had not been easy on the thirty-four-year-old major. Due to the intense North Vietnamese infiltration into his tactical area of responsibility (TAOR), he had lost two fine lieutenants. My predecessor, Lt. John Slater, had fallen to his death from a jungle penetrator, an extract apparatus designed to lift one man at a time out of the jungle and into a helicopter hovering as much as several hundred feet above the battle. Slater's team had been in danger of being overrun by a numerically superior NVA force. After allowing all his men to be lifted to safety, he tried to get on the jungle penetrator with his platoon sergeant so as not to be left alone on the ground. That didn't work out, and Slater fell several hundred feet to his death. In the history of Marine Corps Force Recon, the unit had never been in a bigger fight than they were in under Roger Simmons's command. The challenge was testing him as well as his men.

Larry Beck was the second lieutenant to die on patrol during Simmons's command. His team killed an NVA paymaster and escaped with some very important documents, plus the money. An enraged platoon of NVA caught the recon team in a draw and killed Beck, Private First Class Rose, and a navy corpsman named Pearce. A teenage private by the name of Heineneier braved heavy enemy fire to retrieve the team's only radio from Rose's body. His unselfish act saved the lives of his teammates, Sergeant Karkos and Corporal Spangler. First Force didn't lack credibility because the men weren't brave; it was because the men lacked experience and the proper equipment. Simmons recognized that better equipment would be needed to get his teams in and out of enemy-controlled territory. He was totally committed to finding a way to win. Simmons had been close to Beck and Slater, and their loss devastated him. Therefore, getting close to our new group of young lieutenants was not easy for the major. With rumors circulating internationally that the United States was pulling out of the war, his job of sending good men into enemy-infested jungles to do the impossible was becoming more difficult by the day. So in the spring of 1969, he had some revolutionary equipment secretly designed.

Although privately Simmons worried over the poor support his men received in the field, he always maintained his loyalty to his superiors. Concerning us, the new crop of lieutenants that had showed up almost overnight, Simmons was going to have to break the ice quickly. The stage was being set for a meeting. However, it would not take place until the lieutenants had a chance to compare notes about what kind of support they thought the major would really give them in the field.

The intensity of the patrols had caused our friendship and respect for one another to come together quickly among the lieutenants. Miller and Rollings ordered Recline and Lunch Meat to stand down and relax for the evening. The lieutenants' tent reverberated with the sound of Janis Joplin wailing at the top of her lungs about Bobby

McGee. Captain Williams had made sure a couple of cases of ice-cold beer made it to our tent, and the party had begun. It was a night during which we would all get to know one another. The beer and the music flowed freely.

Wayne Rollings shared his background as a former Marine Corps drill instructor. He was married and the father of an infant daughter. As good a Marine as Wayne was, he never placed himself above the rest of us. He was a brother all the way.

Jim Ritchie talked about his experiences on the radical campus at the University of California at Berkley, where he had spent four years. The radical students put so much pressure on the college administration that he was not allowed to wear his Marine Corps dress-blue uniform to graduation. I could really relate to Jim's experiences, because San Francisco State had been just as bad.

Ric Miller talked about arriving in Vietnam in 1965, just barely eighteen years old. He was a free spirit and loved living on the edge. He admitted, though, that he had lost touch with what was happening back home in the States. Ric and I had grown up about forty miles from each other in central California.

Randy Champe, a former tank officer, was on his second tour, quietly avenging the death of a recon Marine, and his best friend, Rob Barnes. Barnes and Randy had served together with the ROTC unit at the University of New Mexico. Champe was always busy building furniture for the officers' tent out of old ammunition crates. We were all partying, but Randy was partying and building. He was the quiet one among the lieutenants. He was our audience because the rest of us were crazy and noisy.

After chugging a couple of beers, Bob Hansen, the company communications officer, let it be known that he took his job of keeping the communications link between the teams in the field and the command bunker very seriously. He wanted to know immediately if a team had a problem with its radios. He and Champe were also college ROTC buddies from the UNM. Like Rollings, Hansen was married and had a newborn son. When he tried to get serious about our radios, Miller told him to shut up and drink. Bob just smiled, tilted back his head, and chugged another beer while Janis sang about her Mercedes-Benz.

Lynn Lowder had been an enlisted Marine and close friend of John Slater, the lieutenant who had fallen to his death from the jungle penetrator. He and Slater had been selected for and attended Officers Candidate School together. Slater died a couple of weeks before Lowder reported into the company. He was, however, reporting in when the remnant of Lieutenant Beck's team was returning from its ill-fated patrol. Lowder took over Beck's platoon, and after witnessing firsthand what the NVA could do to a recon team, he had a healthy respect for his foe.

I was the last one to share my background, but by the time the attention was turned on me, nobody really gave a damn where I came from; the beer and the music had taken their toll. We were all just having a good time. So I decided to do my impersonation of "Paco," the Cuban hijacker. I used my best Latin accent to narrate a fouled-up airliner takeover. I put on some sunglasses that were on the bar and went into my act. I said, "I am Paco, and this is a jack-high. Put all your crap in the bag, and don't give me any money or jewelry." The deeper I went into the Paco routine, the more of Paco they wanted. So I obliged them. Clearly, we were an intellectual bunch. From that night on I was no longer Bill; I was Paco.

The next day, Sunday, the major gave the company the day off because he could see that the stress level was very

high among his men. The lieutenants hung out together in
their tent. It was time for some serious talk among the
seven of us. We knew that we were in over our heads in
our battle with the NVA. First Force Recon was not meant
to be a tactical unit. We weren't equipped to be taking on
company- and battalion-size enemy units. But that's what
we had been doing, and if we were going to take on the big
boys, then we had to have the support. The confidence
level between Major Simmons and his lieutenants was
going to have to improve. After chewing on the issues all
day long, we decided to ask the major for a meeting. We
unanimously agreed we needed to talk, so we sent word
through Captain Williams. The meeting was set for that
very night in our tent.

Miller kicked off the meeting by asking the major why
the team's reports from the field were not being believed.
Simmons hesitated, and when he saw the eyes of the rest
of the lieutenants riveted on him, he knew he had to answer. Simmons began, "There was a period of time when
1st Force wasn't being employed properly. Doctrinally,
we are the deep reconnaissance unit that serves the Marine
Amphibious Force. For a time, we lost sight of our mission. Our teams became loose, running battalion recon
missions, and we gave up our autonomy. Now that we
work for the right people, that has all changed. These
past few weeks, I have had the opportunity to observe
this group of lieutenants in the field, and I respect your
courage and integrity."

The one question that burned in the hearts of the lieutenants, and had been discussed the most, was not being
asked, so I decided to roll the dice on my future in the
company. I looked the major in the eye and respectfully
asked, "Sir, if we need an emergency extract, and we ask
for one, will you come and get us out?" Simmons thought

for a moment and, making eye contact with each lieutenant, he replied, "Yes, I will." The answer was straight from his heart, and everyone in that tent knew he meant it. The ice was broken, and something good began to happen with the 1st Force Recon Company that night. We sensed that Simmons's commitment to his young lieutenants was real. Our greatest fear, that of being left behind and captured, had been dealt with. The covenant between the major and the lieutenants had been made. Now we would have to act on our commitment to that covenant and one another. A new unity of command was being forged; our "covenant" could make 1969 one of the most successful years in the history of the 1st Force Recon Company.

The next day, late in the afternoon, on Major Simmons's command, Recline was inserted back into the base camp area. The team's LZ was an abandoned fire support base called Cutlass located on Hill 551. All the vegetation had been cleared off the top of the hill for U.S. artillery pieces, which had supported an infantry operation in 1968 called Taylor Common. The NVA normally guarded old American artillery bases, so the air wing insisted on prepping the zone with bombs and rockets. The preemptive air strike had failed to move the NVA off the hill. Recline's insert helicopter took thirty-two bullets on the way into the LZ and nearly crashed. The eight-man team poured down the ramp at a dead sprint onto the smoky, bombed-out fire support base. Visibility was no more than a few feet as fires from the air strike still raged. The thick smoke saved the Marines from being gunned down by the NVA, who were tucked away in the bunkers that covered the hill. The air strikes had temporarily stunned and blinded the enemy, but the sight of eight Force Recon Marines in their midst brought them back to life.

Recline barely made it into an old bomb crater before

they found themselves in a huge firefight with a couple hundred North Vietnamese Army soldiers. From my position as tail-end Charlie, I encountered two NVA soldiers emerging out of the dark gray haze, firing their weapons at almost point-blank range into the departing helicopter. I dove into the bomb crater as a trail of machine-gun fire skipped across the dusty ground and headed toward me. From the air, a helicopter gunship pilot warned Miller over the radio that he had well over one hundred enemy coming up the hill from the south toward the recon team.

Major Simmons, monitoring Recline's situation from the command bunker, decided that he needed to get in a chopper and circle over the battle to best direct his men. Within minutes, he had boarded a Huey gunship that was waiting on the tarmac at An Hoa. Simmons was determined that Recline would have the best support he and the Marine Corps could offer, but prospects for the team grew very dim when all attempts at landing an extract chopper to remove the outnumbered Marines were beaten back by heavy enemy fire. We were sure that the NVA wanted to discourage further reconnaissance penetration into the area.

Recline had a solid lineup with Taylor, the point man, and Private First Class Jones taking the east side of the crater. Ayers had the secondary radio and stayed with me on the north side. Miller kept the primary radioman, Rumpf, with him, to the south. Private First Class Castro, a kid who had already signed a professional baseball contract with the Phillies before leaving for Nam, held down the west flank with Corporal Rush. The antiaircraft fire from several enemy positions was so accurate that we were without air support for the first half hour of the battle. The eight of us used up nearly forty hand grenades and most of our ammunition just to keep from being overrun in the first round of the battle.

Simmons's command chopper arrived over the battle just as the first flight of fixed-wing delivered a napalm strike on the north side of the hill. Ayers and I hugged the bottom of the bomb crater searching for oxygen and relief from the heat of the blast. A second strike sent the two of us crawling toward the center of the crater when the heat began to overwhelm us. Hot ashes began to burn holes in our jungle utilities. The smoke cut visibility to just a few feet.

Miller, seeing the sag in our perimeter, yelled, "You gotta stay over there, the choppers are telling us you've got a platoon of NVA working their way up that draw."

Seeing the M-79 grenade launcher attached to Castro's backpack, I crawled over and grabbed the weapon. I also got a bandolier of high-explosive (HE) rounds from the bewildered private first class. Then I headed back to the north side of the perimeter as Ayers yelled to the rest of the Marines to give him all their M-79 rounds. With nearly one hundred high-explosive rounds in a pile, Ayers smiled at me and said, "Let's give 'em hell, Lieutenant." Ayers laid down a base of fire from his weapon of choice, the M-14, and I leaned over the rim of the crater and fired the high-explosive rounds down the length of the draw, and that sent the advancing enemy running for cover. For an hour, I made my way around Recline's perimeter, arcing M-79 rounds like mortar rounds just outside the perimeter, keeping the NVA from advancing on the bomb crater.

The heavy ground-to-air machine-gun fire drove the Huey gun birds to higher altitudes. This prevented our getting the kind of close air support we needed to keep the NVA from overrunning our position. The enemy was using Recline as bait in an attempt to shoot down some U.S. aircraft.

Two other factors began to become a problem. The 1st

Marine Division Air Wing had major battles raging all over their tactical area of responsibility: the 5th Marines were into a big battle in Antenna Valley; the 1st Marines were into heavy contact with a division-size unit on Go Noi Island, ten miles west of Da Nang; 1st Recon Battalion had two teams in need of air support and emergency extracts on Charlie Ridge. And to compound that critical situation, everybody was running out of daylight.

When the enemy advanced to almost within grenade-throwing range of the perimeter, Miller went on the offensive. He yelled at Ayers and me, "Cover me," then crawled out of the bomb crater to where he thought the grenade had come from. Sure enough, he found a bunker, and just as he started to fire point-blank into the defensive position, out came the barrel of an AK-47 firing on full automatic. Miller pulled his face away from the muzzle of the weapon and rolled backward. "Throw me a grenade," he yelled. Private First Class Castro thought his lieutenant had said, "Throw a grenade," and started to pull the pin on one of his M-26s. Miller, seeing Castro fumbling with the pin, screamed, "Don't *throw* that grenade! Throw *me* a grenade with the pin in it." With that, Castro, the baseball player, threw a perfect strike to Miller, who pulled the pin and delivered the grenade into the bunker, silencing the enemy inside forever.

By then, the air wing had made some decisions as to its priorities, and support of Recline was to be dropped. Escape and evade was the next step for a recon team that was unable to gain control of its extract LZ. When the word came from Major Simmons to escape and evade, Miller was ready. His four years in Vietnam had taught him well, and he wasn't leaving the high ground to be hunted down like a dog by a pack of pissed-off NVA. He grabbed the radio receiver and yelled, "Negative. We ain't running for it; the terrain is too steep, and they know we're here. We're making our stand right from where we are. Over."

Simmons began to lobby the air wing from his command bird, saying, "Somebody has got to try to go in there and get them out." After Simmons's transmission, a calm voice came over the radio.

"Recline, get ready; we're coming in to get you right where we dropped you off, do you copy?"

In disbelief, Miller yelled into the handset, "Roger. We are moving to that position now." Then Miller rose up, waving his arm and yelling, "The chopper is coming in. Let's go." Over the rim of the bomb crater, the Marines came, firing wildly in every direction. The NVA, thinking Recline was trying to escape on foot, threw everything they had at the Marines as they dashed across the open hillside. Suddenly a CH-46 helicopter speared through the smoky haze and landed just thirty meters ahead of the advancing Marines. While Miller and I laid down a base of fire, the team piled onto the big bird. I mowed down one enemy soldier who tried to charge the chopper. Then, diving for the tailgate, I crawled up the ramp, but the chopper began to bounce violently off the ground as Miller tried to get on board. Meanwhile, the pilot took a round through the glass bubble surrounding the cockpit but waited patiently for the crew chief's signal that the whole team was aboard. At the last possible second, I reached off the tailgate and caught Miller by the wrists. Then, with the crew chief's help, I pulled Miller into the chopper. Instantaneously, the pilot gunned the engines, and the chopper lifted off the hill, barely clearing the jungle canopy. Hundreds of enemy bullets went skyward, and over thirty impacted the CH-46, nearly bringing it down. But the courage and bold action of two Marine Corps CH-46 helicopter pilots saved our lives that day.

Marine demonstration brawl

Author Bill Peters (at center of photo, his back to the camera and hand raised) struggles with antiwar protesters in an effort to protect the Marine Corps recruiters at San Francisco State College, March 1968.

The author's family in a farewell toast, August 1968, prior to his going on active duty in the Marine Corps and subsequent deployment to Vietnam. (Left to right) The author; his mom, Lucille; his dad, Bill, Sr.; and his sister, Jan.

Outstanding Force Recon Marine Sergeant D. Mormon, whose faith in God was a real inspiration to the company.

(Left to right) PFC Adams, the author, and PFC Horn. The author trained Adams and Horn to run point for their team, Hanover Sue. The two teenagers were lethal to any NVA who got in their way in the bush.

(Left to right) Lieutenants Tim Ready, Lynn Lowder, Jim Ritchie, and Wayne Rollings. Rollings, a career Marine, rose to the rank of major general.

(Left to right) Lieutenants Steve Corbett, Lynn Lowder, Ric Miller, and Bill Peters. We worked hard in the field and did our best to play hard in the rear.

Lieutenant Randy Champe (left) with Lynn Lowder. Champe served as a tank commander his first tour in Vietnam before volunteering for 1st Force Recon Company.

Lynn Lowder's team testing the 140-foot cable ladder (stretched beneath and behind the chopper), An Hoa, SVN, spring 1969.

The first test
of the Special Patrol
Insert/Extract (SPIE)
rig, June 1969.

NVA officer captured in the Que Son Mountains by the author, Sergeant Eugene Ayers, PFC Adams, and PFC Horn, July 1969.

(Left to right) Lieutenants Bill Peters and Lynn Lowder on August 9, 1969, the day before their successful prisoner grab of an NVA officer deep in enemy-controlled territory.

Lynn Lowder and I showing our commanding officer, Major Roger Simmons, the AK-47 we took from an NVA soldier during a prisoner grab.

General Ormond R. Simpson, commanding officer, 1st Marine Division, conducting an award ceremony for 1st Force Recon Company on Hill 34, September 1969.

On patrol in the Thuong Duc Corridor, December 1969, Sergeant Eugene Ayers (center, in rain gear and beret) is flanked by Corporal Rumpf (left), PFC Adams (right), and Corporal Rush (rear).

(Left to right) Lieutenants Bill Peters, Jim Ritchie, Ric Miller, and Lynn Lowder at Miller's wedding in San Francisco, March 1970.

Ironically, the pilots' names were 1st Lt. Bill Peters and 1st Lt. Tripp Miller. To get us off Hill 551, they risked their lives and careers by violating the Marine air wing's standard operating procedure. Concerning that day on Hill 551, Peters and Miller in the air and a God in heaven saved Recline.

A haunting silence hung over the briefing tent at the 1st Force compound. Miller and I sat among the other lieutenants, exhausted, with blackened faces and jungle utilities mixed with smoke, sweat, and dirt. Captain Williams announced the major's arrival with the customary call to attention. Simmons quickly stated, "That was a real bitch out there today, and I am convinced that prepping the zone before insert doesn't work anymore because it advertises that a recon team insert is taking place, and the NVA set up to kick our butts. The air wing has to change its standard operating procedure, and I have already delivered that message to them. What they did for us today, pulling Recline off Hill 551, was outstanding, but I'd rather not get into those shoot-outs in the first place. That is not our mission." Simmons stopped for a minute and stared at the ceiling of the tent as though in deep thought. Then he smiled and said, "We're all going into Da Nang to pay the wing a visit at their officers club tomorrow night. We need to get to know those guys. Hell, they're getting shot at as much as us. Maybe we can put our heads together with the flyboys and figure out a better plan. We know after today they sure don't lack guts."

Simmons had radioed ahead to the Marine air wing at Marble Mountain that he and his men were coming to party, and a jeep and a six-by truck from the air wing pulled up on the tarmac shortly after we landed. Simmons and Captain Williams jumped into the jeep while the lieutenants piled into the back of the truck. Having left the company at the An Hoa in the good hands of the NCOs, Simmons and his men were out for a night on the town. First Force boldly entered the heavily sandbagged air wing officers club like a bunch of gunfighters out of the Old West. Simmons and Williams burst through the swinging doors shoulder to shoulder with the lieutenants right behind them. The wing officers were ready for their visitors and greeted them with the customary recon growl, "Aruuuuuugah." We recon officers returned the growl, "Aruuuuuugah," and the party began.

The younger officers gravitated to one another and began to exchange team and aircraft call signs. Gallons of drinks were poured and a lot of handshakes exchanged that first hour. It was the first time either unit had seen the other without their game faces. "That was your team down there," one pilot could be heard saying to Wayne Rollings.

Miller and I searched for our namesakes who had rescued Recline off Hill 551. Before long, the four of us had found each other. While shaking hands with pilots Peters and Miller, Ric said, "That was an incredible job you guys did for us yesterday. I've got to buy you a drink."

Tripp Miller responded, saying, "You don't know the half of it. We were low on fuel and didn't have clearance to land, but there were so many bad guys around you on that hill, we knew you wouldn't have lasted much longer." Peters, the pilot, said, "I took a round through the glass in the cockpit that grazed my ankle. I don't know if I could have waited much longer. There were so many muzzle flashes when we were in the air, I couldn't begin to count them."

I ordered a couple of beers for the pilots, handed them the open bottles, and added, "You guys are really named Peters and Miller? That's unbelievable. We owe you big-time."

"You owe us nothing. We were just doing our job," Tripp Miller interjected. With those few words between us, we toasted each other and drank up. Our brotherhood as Marines had been confirmed. We were what the Marine Corps called the great "Air and Ground Team."

Meanwhile, Simmons and Williams made their way over to the senior officers' table and were in the process of ordering a round of drinks for the Marine air wing commander and his staff. About eight of them were seated around a big round table that was already covered with beer bottles and drink glasses. At one point, all the noise stopped dead long enough for us all to hear Simmons bellow, "Now wait a minute, stud." Every eye in the place turned on the wing commander's table. Simmons and his wing counterpart had assumed the wrist wrestling position, eyeball to eyeball. They were locked in mortal combat across that big table, both draped over it to their waists. The wing commander, a colonel, shouted, "Now!" and each man, almost forehead to forehead, attempted to pin the other's hand to the table. The table began to shake and drinks spilled as the two officers struggled violently to win the well-orchestrated pissing contest. Finally Simmons prevailed, grinding the back of the colonel's hand into the tabletop. The victory was followed by a loud *"Aruuuugah!"* by the major, one that evoked an even louder *"Aruuuugah!"* from the lieutenants. Simmons's voice grew louder with victory. Somehow the wrist wrestling had become his rite of passage, one giving him the right to speak frankly to the higher-ranking wing commander.

The major began to state his position on the prepping of his recon teams' landing zones. "It's not just your aircraft at stake, Colonel, it's the lives and missions of entire 1st Force Recon teams. We can't keep announcing ourselves by arriving over our LZ with two CH-46s, circling for a half hour, prepping the zone, and expect to get into an enemy-controlled area without being compromised. You have got to change your tactics."

The colonel was taking in all Simmons was saying without answering.

By that time, both the wing and the recon lieutenants had gathered around the senior officers' table. The young pilots began to speak up. Whether it was the beer or the frustration of risking their lives trying to land in the usually hot recon LZs was not clear. One by one, they began to address the colonel. Tripp Miller kicked it off by saying, "Sir, I think we ought to try to slip into the zones without the prep for a while. Just to see if it works. We can let the backup chopper circle and fake inserts away from our primary LZ and see if we can sneak in the back door. I think it's worth a try."

Another pilot spoke up: "Yeah, let's try it."

Sensing total insurrection beginning, the colonel assumed control of his men. He said, "Okay, now this isn't the time to make the decision, but I'm willing to take it up the flagpole for discussion. But that won't happen overnight."

Simmons seized the moment and said, "That's okay, sir, just as long as we are trying to get it changed, but the quicker the better."

The wing lieutenants, gracious hosts, treated us recon lieutenants to champagne. Lt. Dave Hundley passed out the club's finest crystal, delicate champagne flutes that were used only on occasions such as the annual gala celebration of the Marine Corps' birthday. The glasses were more usually found in the hands of generals and high-ranking civilian officials such as U.S. congressmen. Hundley, a CH-46 pilot of unquestioned courage, was the pilot who had pulled Rollings and me out of the elephant grass when Lunch Meat was surrounded by NVA two weeks earlier.

About fifteen lieutenants formed a circle, holding out the graceful champagne flutes while Hundley, a bottle in each hand, filled them to overflowing. Then we raised our glasses and sang "The Marine Corps Hymn." Hundley proposed the toast, "To the Corps, the wing, and Force Recon. Aruuuuuuugah!" We downed the champagne. Then Force Recon's own Randy Champe and Bob Hansen raised their glasses to their lips, growled, and ate them, spitting the fragments on the rug. The wing lieutenants froze in disbelief. One by one each of the rest of us, recon lieutenants all, took a bite of his flute, spit it out, and growled.

Our challenge did not go unanswered. Hundley led the charge for the wing, biting a huge chunk from his glass and spitting it on the carpet. The rest of the wing lieutenants followed suit.

That night, a bond of mutual respect joined the young wing and recon officers. Our covenant was born in combat and solemnified through ritual; it would carry us through some rough times in the months that lay ahead.

CHAPTER 7

Recon Rock and Roll

Keeping an eye on the political arena during 1st Force Recon's exploits on the battlefield in 1969 is important. The story could be considered as a microcosm of the frustrations endured by the military because of faulty political decisions during the war in Vietnam. First Force's feats in the Central Highlands of Vietnam in 1969 are much more significant when they are projected against the backdrop of the politics surrounding the Vietnam War during that same period.

In the spring of 1969, at a villa tucked away among the wooded rolling hills of a Paris suburb, three negotiators sat in overstuffed leather chairs, sipping tea and debating the future of South Vietnam. The two Vietnamese diplomats listened intently to their American counterpart, veteran diplomat Henry Cabot Lodge, who, in January of 1969, had been shifted from Bonn in what was then the West German Republic to Paris. Lodge, the former ambassador to Saigon, was more than qualified to square off with the Communist negotiators, Xuan Thuy, Hanoi's former minister of foreign affairs. Mrs. Nguyen Thi Binh was from what was said to be the Viet Cong's political arm, the National Liberation Front. Nguyen was married to a Viet Cong regimental commander who had access to the Front Four command group prosecuting the war in the

Central Highlands of South Vietnam. The beautiful and charming Mrs. Nguyen received firsthand information and detailed reports as to how the struggle was progressing from her husband in the field. She knew exactly what the situation in the field was, in terms of the troops' morale, supplies, victories, and defeats. The information she received from her husband was never more than one month old. Nguyen was a veteran Communist diplomat who had served in Moscow, Beijing, and Cairo. The devoted mother of a boy and girl gave the tough-talking National Liberation Front delegation a woman's touch that softened the image of the Viet Cong.

After five months the three negotiators had not progressed beyond discussing the physical shape of the conference table to be used for the talks.

About the same time that this was happening at the Paris Peace Talks, the wheels of change were also turning very slowly on the battlefield. Over six thousand young Americans had already been killed in Vietnam during the first five calendar months of that year. The air wing's SOP for inserting 1st Force Recon into enemy-controlled territory had remained in effect: CH-46 air crews continued to insert teams only after the LZs were "prepped."

The monsoon season was over, and many areas in the Central Highlands of Vietnam were dry. One hot May afternoon, Lieutenants Lowder and Miller were inserted into an LZ that had just been prepped with five-hundred-pound bombs. Lieutenant Hansen, the communications officer, was monitoring the patrol's progress on the radio in the command bunker with Major Simmons and Captain Williams. Hansen listened intently to the quality of the radio signal. Simmons had been concerned that the team might have needed a radio relay to communicate directly with the command bunker. Hansen had no sooner finished saying, "I copy you loud and clear, Grim Reaper," than Lowder's excited voice came up on the radio.

"Ah, Kingfish Six, this is Grim Reaper Six. We've got a fire burning on three sides of us, and we will have to head north to get off our LZ. Over."

Simmons grabbed the handset in response, saying, "Grim Reaper Six, this is Kingfish Six. I roger that. Keep us apprised of your situation. Over."

Lowder said, "Kingfish Six, be advised that we have a wall of about eight-foot-high flames right behind us. Over."

Simmons turned to Captain Williams. "See if the package of helicopters that put Grim Reaper in is still available for an emergency extract."

Lowder and Miller, the wall of flames hungry for their team, began to use their M-16s like sickles to smash through the thick elephant grass, but they could not move the team fast enough, and soon the flames were within a few feet of the rear of the patrol. The thick smoke and intense heat sucked the oxygen out of the Marines' lungs. Lowder let Miller lead the way and got right behind him with the radioman. Lowder began to yell over the radio, "You gotta get us out of here. We can't outrun the fire. Get us out of here. I repeat, this is Grim Reaper, get us out of here!"

Hansen had summoned the rest of the lieutenants from the officers' tent. We were now gathered around the radio in the command bunker listening to Lowder and Miller running for their lives. Rollings, Champe, Ritchie, and I listened as Lowder's voice got more panicky by the minute. Captain Williams continued to speak with wing, which was directing its choppers back to extract Grim Reaper.

Williams grabbed the handset from Simmons and began giving Lowder instructions about the team's extract. Williams calmly said, "Grim Reaper, be advised your ride is on its way. Continue north. The chopper is no more than a minute from setting down on the north edge of that elephant grass, do you copy?" By then the team was on line, weapons over their heads. The men had one hand on the barrel and one on the stock and were using the rifles to smash the grass down in front of them. When the CH-46 landed, the team frantically made its way the last forty feet to the helicopter, whose rotor blast seemed to beat the flames away from the team. Exhausted and dehydrated, Lowder and Miller were the last to climb on the chopper.

The big bird lifted off, and within seconds, flames had engulfed the grassy area under it. There was no celebration from Grim Reaper, only thousand-yard stares as the chopper gained altitude and headed south toward An Hoa. Drenched in their own sweat, the strong smell of smoke coming off them and their equipment, the Marines sat on the floor of the chopper. Simmons was furious when he learned that the bombs that had prepped Grim Reaper's LZ had also started the fire. His appeals to change the insert policy had fallen on deaf ears. Someone up the command structure of the wing was not budging on the issue.

The words to a Janis Joplin song, "Freedom's just another word for nothing left to lose," were blaring from our tent. Stripped to the waist, Lowder and Miller sat on the edge of their racks. Each had a beer in one hand while he sat silently, staring at the floor. Rollings broke the silence when he said, in his Georgia accent, "Damn, that was close for you boys." Miller just shook his head.

Lowder whispered, "Man, I thought we were dead." I sat quietly, just taking it all in. For the first time since I had arrived at 1st Force, I had not been involved in the emergency extract. I turned the music down and just listened. There were long periods of silence in the tent. Joplin's singing could barely be heard in the background. Every few minutes, someone would say something, but no one felt as if he had to reply. Joplin's voice continued to grind away. The songs brought back vivid memories of another battlefield I knew, San Francisco State.

The sun went down, and the lieutenants checked on their platoons, then returned to the tent for cold C rations and more Janis Joplin. Our morale was not real good, but as the music continued, I was reminded of the good times back home. I finally broke the ice when I said in my Paco accent, "I remember when Janis did that song at the Fillmore Auditorium last year. What a night that was. I mean, you think the smoke was heavy on that LZ today? Man, you couldn't see three feet in front of your nose in the Fillmore that night. Stoned hippies, standing room only, and the building was shaking so much it felt like an earthquake."

Miller, who had spent only a few months in the States since 1965, wanted to know more about it. Jim Ritchie began to talk about the good times at U.C. Berkeley, and suddenly, we were no longer in Vietnam. I had them walking the streets of the Haight-Ashbury district, where, from my bedroom window at the fraternity house, I had watched the cultural revolution take place. I was giving my new friends a history—history as seen through Paco's eyes. Miller and some of the others had only read or heard about San Francisco during the late 1960s, but I was taking them into what I had lived.

Sometime during Paco's monologue, one of the lieutenants stopped the Joplin tape and put on Blood, Sweat, and Tears, then a new group. The lead singer crooned, "I lost at love before," and we stopped talking and quietly listened to the song. There was a lot of nostalgia that evening. As the beer flowed and the night wore on, a strange peace returned to the tent. We were learning how to escape the realities of a war that our country no longer wanted to fight. Paco's humor kept things on a light note. Meanwhile, the bond of our relationship continued to be forged in some of the most dangerous kind of combat missions available to young junior officers like us.

My first mail from home reached me early the next day. My letters home had obviously arrived, because someone had received my address. The reality of where I was and what I was doing somehow broke in on me when I read the postmarks and return addresses on the envelopes. The letter from San Francisco was from Pam, and the ones from Livermore were from my mom and sister. I read each letter once and then put them away in my locker box; I felt my edge begin to soften as I read them. A few minutes after putting my mail away, I looked up, and Sergeant Ayers stood in the doorway of the tent. Seconds into the conversation with him, the edge returned. We had a patrol coming up, and it was time to go over our plan. It would be our first patrol with team members from Lieutenant Slater's old 2d Platoon.

Simmons must have passed out orders to every lieutenant, because all the platoon sergeants were descending on the officers' tent. First Force's sergeants were an outstanding group of noncommissioned officers. Rollings had a new sergeant, Mormon, who had tremendous bearing and discipline. Ritchie's platoon sergeant was Joe Crockette, a tall sandy-haired Marine, new to Vietnam but very experienced with recon units back in the States. Champe's sergeant was Theodore Ott. His gravelly voice came from deep within him. Ott had an abundance of patrolling experience. Miller still had not replaced Sanders, his former platoon sergeant. Lowder had inherited Sergeant Karkos, who carried a bullet hole in the biceps as a souvenir of Lieutenant Beck's ill-fated patrol. In 1st Force, the same magic that existed among the lieutenants existed among the platoon sergeants.

Ayers prepared the team for our mission. We had some good men on the team, but months of being without an officer's leadership had given them an unhealthy independence. Ayers warned me that he felt they were resisting his leadership. But we agreed that this was the hand that we had been dealt and we would make the best of it.

I moved cautiously down the ramp of the CH-46 on my first patrol as team leader. Our call sign was Renegade. The LZ was a dry streambed with brush and grass growing out of the parched sand. I moved slowly up the dry bed and then moved the team over to the south bank and knelt, just to listen as the sound of the chopper faded in the distance. I craned my head to make eye contact with Ayers, who was running tail-end Charlie. I grimaced as Ayers crouched down on one knee and gave the team a clenched-fist freeze sign. Damn, I thought, two minutes into the patrol, and we already have a problem. Ayers gave me the move-out sign while he himself stayed put. Ayers used the secondary radio to communicate with me. I was walking third man from the front. The primary radioman signaled me and gave me the handset. Ayers whispered the situation to me, saying, "We have got three following us in the streambed. Let's get a gun bird to fire on them and give us a chance to double-time it the hell out of here."

I requested air support immediately. Within minutes, a Cobra gunship was firing rockets at the enemy, and I ran the team north to lose the enemy. Within seconds, crackling sounds could be heard where the rockets had landed, and Ayers radioed up to me one word, "Fire." After what Lowder and Miller had gone through, I was determined to stay way ahead of the blaze, but not at the risk of being ambushed. I moved the team quickly but carefully, stopping and listening every minute or two for sounds of enemy activity. Renegade had to get out of the streambed if we were to lose the NVA who were tracking us. I also felt that we could be pushed into an ambush if I allowed the team to continue on a predictable route. Force Recon normally did not walk on enemy trails, and we also stayed away from streams, because both environments usually attracted enemy soldiers. The chance of making a point or tail-end Charlie contact in such areas was very strong.

Ayers did not like being hounded by the enemy from the rear. The element of surprise had already been lost, and the dry, sandy streambed made it very hard to disguise Renegade's patrol route. Now his worst fears began to be played out. He spotted at least one other enemy soldier moving quickly along the team's flank. Ayers's heart raced as he aimed his M-14 rifle at the olive-drab-uniformed NVA. He studied his foe's equipment, noting the AK-47 assault rifle was being carried on a jungle strap slung over one shoulder, the barrel horizontal, sweeping from side to side following the movement of his head. Ayers had begun to squeeze the trigger when the word *decoy* entered his mind. He immediately eased off the trigger and slowly turned his head to the rear. Sure enough, he could make out two more silhouettes moving very slowly through the smoke that was now blowing ahead of the fire. Using the crackling sound of the brush fire to disguise the sounds of their movement, the two NVA had moved dangerously close to Ayers. If he had pulled the trigger, his position would have been given away, and the NVA behind him would have poured automatic fire all over him. Ayers began to pray that I would turn the patrol west, away from the flanking action of the enemy.

I was becoming more uncomfortable with the direction of the patrol as I eased Renegade down the streambed. I could sense Ayers's discomfort, so I carefully moved forward toward my point man, a kid named Parrish. Parrish caught my hand signal as his eyes quickly left and then returned to the terrain in front of him. Like all point men, Parrish had been trained to see movement in any direction. I had signaled west, and within two steps, Parrish had the team headed that way.

Ayers's silent prayer had been answered. Even so, Ayers planned to lead the enemy farther up the streambed before doglegging his way back to the team. Leading the enemy on a wild-goose chase was no move for an amateur. Ayers continued to leave just enough sign for the NVA to follow. The two enemy soldiers moved past Renegade's exit point without noticing it. Ayers had covered it well. Now his eyes strained ahead of him to locate the enemy soldier who had moved up the flank a few minutes earlier. Surely, he's setting an ambush, Ayers thought. Finally, he spotted the man crouched in some bushes, waiting patiently for Renegade to surface. It was time for Ayers to go. No Marines were left between the enemy soldier in the ambush position and his two buddies who had been tracking Renegade.

Ayers used the sound of the fire and the dense smoke to move around the two unsuspecting NVA. He could tell that the inevitable was about to happen. Sure enough, within minutes the NVA waiting in ambush opened up on his buddies, killing both of them before either one could even begin to return fire. Ayers moved quickly to rejoin the team.

Renegade had frozen at the sound of the gunfire. My heart sank when I did not hear an M-14 fire in response to the distinctive sound of the AK-47. Picturing Ayers dead somewhere along the streambed, I signaled my radioman to approach me. I keyed the handset a couple of times to get the secondary radioman at the back of the patrol to come up on the net. Relief came over my face when Ayers's voice came over the radio saying, "Be advised, sir, that our NVA friends just had a little accident. Let's get the hell out of here." I motioned to Parrish to move out.

The team began to move up the side of a rocky hill that was sparsely covered with trees and brush. After only one hundred meters, Parrish signaled that there was downhill movement toward the team. At my signal, Renegade moved quietly into a brush-covered draw, and the men took up defensive fighting positions on their bellies. More NVA in olive-drab uniforms, their weapons at the ready position, ran past us in the direction of the streambed. Renegade did not move while the Ho Chi Minh sandals of more than ten NVA passed by at eye level, right in front of the recon team. A fishlike odor from the enemy's clothes and equipment filled the air. When the NVA reached the streambed, they became very quiet, with only occasional low, indistinguishable voices to be heard. Ayers surmised that the larger unit had found the ambush site and were probably being briefed about Renegade's presence in the area by the lone NVA survivor.

With the sun beginning to fall behind the Que Son Mountains to the west, a dark shadow was cast over the area, which further covered Renegade's position. The fire in the streambed continued to burn and was fully visible to the team. But as it began to die out, with only some orange embers glowing, the shadow of the mountains began to overtake it. An unnatural hush fell over the area. I realized the enemy did not know our position, so I decided to stay put. I signaled the radioman to give the command center our position and situation so that Simmons could prepare an air package if we needed help.

In the streambed, after learning of the American reconnaissance presence in the area, the NVA had taken up a defensive perimeter. The lone NVA survivor was probably sitting in a heap on the ground, lamenting the loss of his friends. I doubted if any of his contemporaries were trying to comfort him or even looked in his direction. But I was sure of one thing, and that was that the NVA were real pissed off at us.

We would find out in the months that lay ahead that the area had been teeming with the soldiers from the 2d NVA Division, which, unknown to us, was headquartered less than a thousand meters to the west in the Que Son Mountains. We were messing with something very big, but we just thought the patrol was business as usual. Front Four had been run out of Go Noi Island in recent weeks by Marine infantry. Higher intelligence had evidence that they were now in the Que Son Mountains, but of course, I had no knowledge that Front Four was nearby. At that time, I thought Front Four was a myth. My thought was, if I played my cards right, maybe the team would make it out alive with some important information about the heavy enemy activity in the area.

From his tail-end Charlie position in the shallow ravine, Ayers saw a column of NVA appear on line. They began to fan the glowing embers of the brushfire with coolie hats and pith helmets. They quickly had a flame started and the fire directed up the side of the hill. Their intention was clear to Ayers, who was whispering to me over the radio. With the fire being pushed by a slight breeze toward Renegade's hideaway, I gave the order for the team to crawl slowly to the top of the hill. Probably in fear of ambushing themselves once again, the NVA made no attempt to control the top of the hill, so Renegade soon owned it. Quickly forming a tight defensive position, we watched the NVA fan the fire up the side of the hill. I got on the radio with Simmons. "We are outnumbered, outgunned, and out of daylight." Renegade owned the top of a very big hill, but that was subject to change at any minute.

Simmons called for Spooky, a slow-moving cargo plane owned by the air force. It had more firepower than ten gun birds all firing at the same time, and it could stay on station for hours. "It is going to take about thirty minutes for her to reach you, Renegade," Simmons warned. I gave the team orders not to fire first unless a team member's life was in danger. Ayers controlled one side of the perimeter, and I the other. Silently, we waited as the fire began to die out for lack of fuel. The NVA stopped their advance and seemed to be regrouping for orders. They had moved to within twenty-five meters of Renegade's position. For the first time in hours, Vietnamese voices could be heard. They were either confident that they could wipe out the American intruders or they felt that the team had escaped. We held our breath as the NVA platoon, numbering in the twenties, milled around in the dark, shouting back and forth at one another. They were searching the area that we had just vacated. It had already been burned over by the fire. Their search bought the team just enough time to get Spooky on station.

At Spooky's request, I turned on a strobe light to mark my position. As the NVA turned to look at the bright strobe, a long humming sound came from the heavens, raining down bullets on them like inch-long hailstones. The first burst of fire left a wide trail of death in its path. Half the enemy platoon lay dead or wounded on the hillside. The

other half sprinted down the hill and into the dry streambed. Spooky stayed with us all night. This kept the NVA
away from our position. But at first light, Spooky had to
leave because, in the daylight, it presented NVA antiaircraft weaponry with a very large, slow-moving target.

The NVA, recognizing the team's sudden vulnerability
with Spooky's disappearance, charged the top of the hill.
My point man, Parrish, was struck down by enemy fire.
He and I were standing together challenging the enemy's
assault with M-16s firing on full automatic. Rounds were
dancing against the rocks above our heads when Parrish
was hit. I tossed a grenade in the direction of the enemy's
advance. Parrish lay groaning on the ground as the team
formed a protective base of fire to keep the NVA from advancing and possibly taking Parrish as a POW. With members of the team tending the wounded point man, I got on
the radio and called in more air support. Within seconds,
Renegade had two gun birds circling above her, but heavy
ground fire drove them away. Within minutes, Phantom
jets were making passes over our position. An aerial observer took control of the nape and snake strikes, blasting
the enemy positions.

Once again, the NVA were not letting go of an American
recon unit. Fueled by reports coming out of the Paris Peace
talks and the U.S. news media concerning the Americans'
imminent withdrawal from Vietnam, the word from Hanoi
was "to fight hard until the Americans leave." Front Four
had received orders to conduct a summer offensive that
would be aimed at Da Nang, and one of its tactics was to
hurt the recon teams and discourage their presence in the
Que Son Mountains. With 1st Force Recon pushed out of
the mountains, the NVA would have little trouble massing
troops for the summer offensive. The Hanoi government

felt that any offensive at that time would tend to weaken the Americans' withdrawal plans.

At the culmination of a massive series of air strikes delivered to rescue us, a Marine CH-46 helicopter sat down just off the north side of the rocky hill. I took point. With four of the team members carrying Parrish and with Sergeant Ayers bringing up the rear, I led the team to the chopper. Before the smoke from the air strikes had lifted, Renegade was one thousand feet in the air and headed to 1st Medical Battalion with our wounded point man. The chopper was met on the landing pad by a doctor and several corpsmen, who reassured me, saying, "We got him; he's going to make it, so don't worry." I *was* worried, but there was little time to show it.

I had only one impression during this rash of fires, woundings, and deaths among our recon teams. The Que Son Mountains had not been touched by 1st Force. I noticed that we patrolled around the Que Sons but not *in* the Que Sons; I felt that the NVA were hiding something major up there.

No sooner did Simmons get Renegade out than another team, call sign Short Timer, radioed for help from its position at the base of the Que Sons. Although assigned to Jim Ritchie, Short Timer was being led by his platoon sergeant, Joe Crockette. Crockette, no older than twenty-one years, was caught in dry elephant grass with one dead Marine and several wounded. The NVA had started another fire and were burning the team out when Crockette radioed for help. Tying a yellow air panel onto his back so that air support could identify his position through the smoke hanging over the battle, Crockette manned the "perimeter" by himself because the rest of his men were wounded or dead. Even so, he managed to back the enemy off with automatic fire as his wounded teammates loaded the M-16s and handed them to

Crockette. As the fire grew near his men, the young sergeant moved the bodies of the dead and wounded away from the blaze. Fire seemed to be the enemy's new weapon of choice against 1st Force Recon teams working in the lowlands near the Que Son Mountains.

Crockette fought for his life while the gunships searched through the thick smoke for a glimpse of his recon team. Finally a gun bird spotted the air panel on Crockette's back and directed the CH-46 extract bird, call sign Lady Ace, to sit down close to the Marine's position. Braving the fire, Lady Ace hovered a few feet off the ground as flames licked at her underbelly. Crockette made sure his dead and wounded got on the bird. He then stayed on the ground and joined a company-size reaction force from the Fifth Marines that had been deployed to take on the NVA and destroy them. This concept was called a Stingray operation. It often proved very effective. In that case, the NVA began disappearing back under the jungle canopy, avoiding any confrontation with the Stingray reaction force. Crockette would have to take his revenge another way; the enemy broke contact and ran back into the Que Sons.

At the day's end, having lost one Marine permanently and five others to wounds, Major Simmons and Captain Williams sat in the command bunker, discussing the readiness of the company to begin running missions in the Que Sons and all the way west to the Laotian border if necessary. The III MAF command group was not hinting that 1st Force might be asked to do deeper and even more dangerous missions. Simmons anguished over his ability to support us in the field. There was little question that the men would go when asked; he was determined to find a better way to insert and extract them on such dangerous missions.

One afternoon, a CH-46 helicopter carrying a net full of equipment suspended beneath it by a cargo strap caught

Simmons's eye. He stopped walking and just stared at the chopper. He was spellbound by what he saw. Although he had seen choppers carry gear like that a thousand times before, this time he had a very important vision. He and Captain Williams brainstormed how they could carry a recon team on a strap beneath a CH-46 helicopter. Finally, they agreed to a scheme to sew three-foot-long straps and stagger them along the lower portion of a 140-foot-long cargo strap. They decided that at the end of the staggered straps they would sew in steel D rings. D rings would also be sewn into the Marines' Ranger straps.* Then a nylon rope would be slipped through the Recon Marine's D rings, and with the use of a heavy-duty snaplink, the individual Marines could snap onto the D rings at one of the stations on the cargo strap. The major named the new invention the SPIE rig, or special patrol insert extract rig. The whole idea was ingenious, bordering on nothing less than divine inspiration.

The major dispatched Captain Williams to fly to Okinawa and procure all that was necessary to build the rig. Williams was also provided with a list of equipment that the company needed to do the missions they were being asked to do. Everything from radios to silenced weapons was on that list.

We knew that 1st Force was really getting under the NVA's skin when one afternoon we received a salvo of enemy rocket fire directed at our An Hoa compound. Although nine of the ten rockets landed short of the living area in the compound, one rocket, a dud, had landed right on line with the command bunker. Falling about twenty meters short, it left an eight-foot-long, four-inch-deep scar on the ground, marking the near perfect accuracy of the missile. That was enough for Simmons. He was convinced that 1st Force had been singled out for extinction by the NVA and that it was time to move the company to a safer area. Simmons's and Williams's plan was simple. They would secure permission from III Marine Amphibious Force to move the company toward the coast. Then 1st Force would stand down for one month to train and to replace our dead and wounded. It would also give Williams some extra time on Okinawa to scrounge gear. The training and new equipment would help 1st Force to vigorously patrol into the Que Son Mountains. The company would also be better prepared to run deeper missions that III MAF might want. Simmons's plan met with immediate approval, and he received orders quickly to move the company to Hill 34 near Da Nang, a first-class compound where a good training area already existed. General Nickerson, the commander of III MAF, was taking a personal interest in 1st Force.

A ritual had begun among the lieutenants at An Hoa. The heavier the contact, the riskier the patrols, the louder and wilder the parties in our tent. Although the recent loss of men, both dead and wounded, had made an impression on us, we lieutenants refused to allow our grief to bring us down. We talked a lot about what we were experiencing in the field. Once the compound had been secured for the night, the lieutenants would ritualistically gather in the officers' tent to share their victories and defeats in the bush. There was no competition among us because there were plenty of missions to be run, glory to be had, and the guts to go for it. In the relatively short time we had been together, we had gained respect for each other's unique traits.

---

*A Ranger strap is what we called the harness worn over the shoulders and attached to a cartridge belt at the waist.

The crucible of battle had forged our relationships, and nobody had to impress anybody else in the group.

Once Simmons received his preliminary order to prepare for moving the company, he summoned the lieutenants together to the briefing tent and gave us orders to begin to pack up our platoons. Since all the lieutenants were in from the bush that night, we returned to our tent, and out came the beer and wine. The party was on. We sensed that we had survived a real test at An Hoa. We knew we had the ability to endure the stress of constant danger without succumbing to it. So we were having a graduation party. The Neil Diamond song "Brother Love's Salvation Show" blared from our tent. Of course, Miller and I changed the words to "It's a ragged tent down in old An Hoa." Lowder sang the song over and over until he was hoarse. The six-foot-five-inch farm boy had false teeth, and each time he finished the song, he looked at us and popped his front teeth out with his tongue. Then he would flash us a toothless smile. Miller and I entertained the group with the Paco skit. Champe, Rollings, Hansen, Lowder, and Ritchie were laughing so hard at Paco's exploits, their howls could probably be heard a mile away. Simmons, hearing the roar coming from the lieutenants' tent, probably just smiled and rolled over in his cot and went to sleep. Not many years before, he had been a Force Recon lieutenant, and I am sure he understood what the camaraderie between recon Marines was all about. He never questioned what we did with our own time at night. He had a winning team, and he knew it.

There was a feeling of newness as the sun began to warm the tents in the 1st Force compound. It was Sunday, so no company formation was called. Simmons let the troops sleep in, attend church services, write home, and go to chow. It was unusually quiet in the officers' tent that particular morning. The empty beer cans strewn all over the floor were solid evidence that a good time was had the night before. Unexpectedly, a young private knocked on the flap of the tent. "Who is it?" Rollings growled.

"Sir, it's PFC Garza with the mail."

"Leave it on the bar and get out of here," Miller ordered.

"Yes, sir. Is it okay if I move some of these beer cans so I can make room for it?"

"Sure. Go ahead, and then get out of here," Miller groaned.

The temptation of the mail was enough of an incentive to get me out of the rack. Within minutes of the private's departure, I was up, rummaging through the assortment of packages and envelopes. Three were for me. A package from my mom, a letter from Pam, and another letter from Lee Wallace, who was finishing his flight training in Beeville, Texas. First I dug through Mom's package, finding the .38-caliber Colt snub-nosed revolver and a can of Mace I had requested. It was hidden in a box of dry oatmeal. "All right, Mom!" I could not control my enthusiasm, so I announced to the whole tent what my mom had accomplished in breaking at least twelve federal gun laws by sending me the pistol. "Hey, wake up. You got to see this pistol and Mace I got for our prisoner grabs," I hollered.

Someone in the back of the tent threw an empty beer can at me and yelled, "Shut up, Paco, and go back to sleep, or we are going to 'jack high' you."

I gave up on getting anyone to check out my new toys. I grabbed the box and letters. Then I retreated to my rack in the back of the tent. The information in Pam's envelope read like a form letter. I couldn't feel any soul in it. She must have felt duty-bound to write. I tried not to care; I still looked forward to hearing from her. There was still a spark there, but it was not as strong as it once had been.

Lee's letter was full of information. He had landed on an aircraft carrier and trained with the Marine Corps in close ground-to-air support techniques. He reassured me that he would fly at treetop level to cover my recon team. I smiled at my best buddy's enthusiasm. Just three more months, and Lee could be flying a Phantom over my team, I thought. The odds of both of us making it back alive were not very good, but we were warriors destined for that kind of adventure. So I dismissed the fears from my mind. For the first time since I had arrived in Vietnam just six weeks earlier, I felt an unusual peace in my soul. I could not pinpoint the changes going on inside of me, but San Francisco State and the campus politicians seemed so trivial. And I was convinced that dwelling on a girlfriend could get me killed. I was completely committed to breaking my emotional bond with Pam. Vietnam, 1st Force Recon, and the men I was serving with were becoming my life, and I loved it.

Reaching back into my mother's package, I noticed a new *Life* magazine. The cover announced a section called "Those Who Died in Vietnam This Week." I thumbed my way through the magazine, finally stopping on the Vietnam article. Several pages were covered with service photographs. When I happened upon the names and pictures of John Laken, Al Nelson, and Ted Vivillaqua, I dropped the magazine in my lap. I just stared at it. Those guys were friends I had come into country with, and they were already dead. Laken, a graduate of Purdue, was a sharp officer. He and I had gone on liberty in Washington, D.C., many times. Al Nelson had grown up in the Marine Corps. His dad was a sergeant major. Vivillaqua was a graduate of the U.S. Naval Academy, where he had played football. He was brilliant but down-to-earth. There were many cold mornings during our training at Quantico that Vivillaqua had kept all of us laughing with his quick humor. But the thing that had the greatest impact on me was the fact that my friends had all died within their first month in Vietnam, and their deaths were not attributed to direct enemy contact but to mines and booby traps. The thought angered and sickened me.

Slowly I turned the pages of the magazine. I stopped on an article about President Nixon's impending meeting on Midway Island with President Thieu of South Vietnam. According to the article, rumors were circulating that Nixon might tell Thieu that the United States was turning the war over to the South Vietnamese. Worked into the article was a picture of Ambassador Henry Cabot Lodge with his North Vietnamese counterpart in Paris, France, pointing at an odd-looking conference table. I knew that morning, in my gut, that there was about to be a major shift concerning the war and the United States was probably pulling out.

During that quiet Sunday morning, while the 1st Force Recon Company slept, I walked out of the officers' tent and climbed up on the roof of a sandbagged bunker. Facing west, I stared at the enemy mountains and spent a couple of hours in deep thought. I traced my motives for being here in Nam. That had not changed. I knew that being there was part of my destiny. I instinctively knew that someday, if I survived, I would be qualified to shed light on the single most divisive event in U.S. history since the Civil War. Now I had the opportunity, through 1st Force, to work in the secret recesses of the enemy's base camps and entry points into South Vietnam. I could become someone who really had special insight into the Vietnam War. I decided that morning to exploit those circumstances to the maximum. I decided that I really had a chance to avenge the deaths of my friends who were out in the infantry chasing shadows. I knew where the NVA were, and I was being sent after them. Perched on that bunker that quiet Sunday morning, I decided to make my tour really count. At the top of my list was payback to the NVA for friends lost. If I was allowed to live through Vietnam, I felt that it would take some kind of divine intervention. As I jumped down from the bunker, I recalled my father's words: "Bill, don't ever forget your family, and don't forget God."

CHAPTER 8

The Que Son Fandango

Rollings and I had decided to team up on another patrol and were headed toward Base Area 112. Our chopper was flying at about twenty-five hundred feet. Jim Ritchie, the U.C. Berkeley grad, was in a second CH-46 with his team, Report Card, flying at the same altitude. This was the standard recon air package, with two 46s flying in tandem toward their objective. The NVA knew that soon the 46s would begin to circle while their zones were being prepped by air strikes and rocket fire. As the two choppers moved up Antenna Valley, just south of An Hoa, .50-caliber machine-gun fire coming off the Que Son Mountains struck Ritchie's 46, sending it on a downward spiral. Rollings and I watched in horror through an open port in our chopper as Ritchie's bird continued its dive, stabilized at about three hundred feet, then plunged nose first into the valley floor, killing the pilot and copilot instantly.

Ritchie and Report Card were thrown around inside the big bird like a bunch of rag dolls. The smell of aviation fuel filled the chopper as he regained consciousness. He could hear the moans of his men. He took inventory: his point man had a broken arm, the radioman a broken leg, and several of the team members were in shock. Ritchie himself was barely able to breathe because of his broken ribs. He pulled himself to his feet, grabbed a radio, and made a situation report. Ritchie, Raven Six, strained to speak to Hostage Bear, a Cobra helicopter pilot. Before Ritchie could report, he began to take small-arms fire from a nearby tree line. AK-47 rounds began to impact the downed chopper.

Rollings and I were monitoring Ritchie's radio transmission with the Cobra pilot. When Rollings heard that the team was alive and that they were taking fire, he rushed up front to talk with his pilots. Rollings yelled, "They're alive and taking fire from that tree line to the north. Get us down there so we can get them out." The CH-46 pilots, Lieutenant Hundley and Lieutenant Stevens, knew their contemporaries had died on impact. Visibly choked up, they began a tight spiral down toward the chopper wreckage and a sure firefight in the valley below. The unspoken covenant between the recon Marines and the helicopter pilots was once again being tested.

Cobra gunships worked over the tree line to the north as our CH-46 landed near the crash site. Aviation fuel had spread through the ankle-deep water on the valley floor for a ten-meter radius around the downed bird. Rollings and I removed Report Card's wounded by carrying them onto our 46. Once the medevac was complete, the 46 with the wounded lifted off, and Lunch Meat set up a perimeter around the wreckage.

While NVA infantry continued to snipe at the crash site, we kept the covenant and went to work recovering the dead pilots whose bodies were trapped in the 46's crushed cockpit. When Rollings and I entered the wreckage, we saw that the 46 would have to be raised up so that we could crawl under the cockpit and release the pilots from their seats. After finding a nylon mail strap, Rollings got on the radio and requested Hostage Bear to get another 46 so it could lift the wreckage and we could extract the pilots.

In minutes, Rollings had hooked one end of the nylon cable to the wreckage and handed the other end to the crew chief of another 46 hovering a few feet above the downed bird.

Suddenly AK-47 rounds started impacting all around our perimeter. One spark from the incoming rounds would be enough to detonate the aviation-fuel-laden water surrounding the recon team. Rollings's plea to silence the enemy fire was answered within seconds as a Phantom jet dove from the sky and unloaded 250-pound bombs on the distant tree line. Working feverishly as the wreckage was lifted, Rollings and I scrambled under the crushed cockpit, freeing one pilot and dragging his body to safety. Once again, the wreckage was lifted; we slipped under the cockpit, reached through the shattered glass, and tried desperately to undo the copilot's seat belt. "I can't get it," I yelled.

"I don't know how long they can keep this bird off the deck. Hurry!" Rollings hollered back.

"I've almost got it," I said.

"It's coming down, Paco. Get out of there," Rollings yelled. Rollings slipped back under the cockpit with me.

"He's free, Wayne, let's get him out of here," I yelled.

Just as we pulled the dead pilot clear from under the tons of twisted metal, down it all came. The force of the wreckage hitting the ground created a wave of aviation-fuel-saturated water strong enough to body-surf the two of us into a nearby embankment. The ride surprised the both of us, and we belatedly realized how close we had come to being crushed. The mission was accomplished as Lunch Meat carried the bodies of the pilots onto another 46. As a Phantom jet unloaded its napalm over the wreckage, creating a huge orange fireball, our fuel-soaked team was flown out of Antenna Valley and back to An Hoa. That ensured that none of the chopper's weapons or equipment would fall into enemy hands.

That action signaled the beginning of the end of the wing's standard operating procedure for inserting Force Recon teams. The loss of the two pilots and the recovery of their bodies further strengthened the bond between Force Recon and the wing. Pilots and recon team leaders would work closely together in the days ahead, with great results.

First Force's new boss, III Marine Amphibious Force, wanted to run its recon teams out to the Laotian border on a highly sensitive set of missions. The lieutenants were convinced the real enemy presence was between the Que Sons and Base Area 112, that is, much closer to Da Nang and important military installations than the brass would like to admit. With the downing of Ritchie's chopper right below the Que Sons, plus all the rest of the action involving that region, it had become very difficult to ignore the obvious: the NVA's presence in those mountainous areas was overwhelming. Major Simmons was determined to keep the importance of the Que Sons in front of III MAF and General Nickerson. After all, Force Recon blood had been shed near there without 1st Force's ever really patrolling in the Que Sons themselves.

Right before we left An Hoa, there was a lull in the number of patrols we ran. All the lieutenants were out of the bush at the same time for nearly two weeks, and like most healthy young men, we sought out and found something fun to occupy our time, so we arranged to train our teams near Alligator Lake, which was located a mile above our camp, just on the edge of some very questionable and heavily foliated mountains. Questionable because everybody seemed to leave the area alone. The reason for this hands-off approach was probably the Red Cross hospital that occupied an old French resort at one end of the lake near the base of the mountains. Ritchie had gotten some care from the German nurses stationed there after his chopper crash. He and Champe had gotten to know them fairly well, so soon we all were stopping by the hospital regularly for the treatment of fabricated symptoms. Our favorite affliction was intestinal worms, because frequent stool samples had to be delivered to the beautiful nurses, and the test results usually took several weeks. That gave us something to look forward to.

Major Simmons must have been pleased with all the "training" we were doing around Alligator Lake, because he didn't question the amount of time we spent there. We would set up an M-60 machine gun and train it on the mountain while we swam and horsed around in the lake. We did do some training, but most of the time, the nurses and the lake doubled as an in-country R & R center.

The whole setup was too good to be true. One morning, we showed up at the hospital in full force only to be greeted with the news that the NVA had slipped into the nurses' quarters the night before and kidnapped our beautiful German nurses. We never really called them by name. They were just friends who babied us a little and were kind to us. The six of us lieutenants just sat around the lake that day and stared at the mountains, wondering if we would ever run into our German friends again. There was something final about their disappearance. Though we had standing orders for the next few months to be on lookout for them when we were in the bush, they never surfaced. Although we had known them for only those few weeks, it was hard for us not to want to take their disappearance personally as payback from the NVA. It was as if the mountains had swallowed them up, and reality had replaced our boyish fling.

While the company was packing up for the move to Hill 34, I was packing up to man a mountaintop observation post (OP) just across Antenna Valley and facing the Que Son Mountains. My new call sign was Hanover Sue. The team was to spend ten days on the observation post, which was well within the range of the 175mm artillery guns at An Hoa.

When the CH-46 touched down on the bald ridgeline, I noted that the only way to attack the position would be from the east end of the narrow ridge. A trail ran along the ridge down the hill to a village that was protected by South Vietnamese Army forces (ARVN). The north, south, and west sides of the hill were sheer cliffs, dropping several hundred feet into some very deep ravines. Other than being vulnerable to mortar rounds, the observation post seemed easily defendable. I checked my fields of fire on the east end of the hill, and after dark I set up a couple of M-60 machine guns to defend the position.

Having my team out in the open on that hilltop seemed strange after hiding in the jungle on every other patrol. I did not like losing the element of surprise; given the choice, I preferred being the hunter rather than the hunted. Early on the first morning of our mission, Sergeant Ayers and I were sitting on the pinnacle of the observation post. We were looking across Antenna Valley at a trail that followed the base of the Que Son Mountains. The trail was visible from the OP for several hundred meters by using a powerful M-1 spotter scope. To Ayers's amazement, he picked up the movement of a large group of NVA using the trail. "Look at this, Lieutenant," Ayers said as he handed me the scope. I crushed a flying ant that landed on my cheek, smiled as he brought the scope into focus, and began to study the large column of enemy soldiers. It was payback time for Laken, Nelson, and Vivillaqua!

"Okay, Sergeant Ayers, let's get some artillery fire on the little bastards," I growled. Within seconds, I was on the radio talking with the 175mm artillery battery guns at An Hoa. The trail Ayers had discovered was not on the map, so I asked the artillery battery for a white phosphorus spotter round to be fired on a specific grid coordinate near the trail. The spotter round landed within a couple of hundred meters of the trail, but the column of NVA ignored it and continued marching. I adjusted my fire, bringing the second spotter round close enough to the trail to make the enemy run. My next words to the artillery battery were "Give me high explosive and fire for effect."

Ayers, his eye glued to the spotter scope, reported, "Sir, we have twenty-five NVA in the open. That round you just fired landed at the end of the column, taking out at least five or six of them. They were vaporized on impact." There was no movement on the trail for the rest of the morning. After hours of observing no movement on the trail, Ayers and I were ready to chalk up our early-morning sighting as just a fluke.

Flying ants covered the top of the OP, and the lack of shade on the bald hilltop made it even more uncomfortable. Because of the heat, I told Ayers that the men were allowed to wear tiger stripe or green Marine Corps–issue shorts and strip to the waist. Flak jackets and helmets were to be within arm's reach, no matter where the men were on the hill; mortar fire was a distinct possibility. Although the OP had never been overrun by the enemy, there had been nighttime probes.

Late in the afternoon, Ayers, who had been studying the Que Son Mountains through the spotter scope, once again picked up a large number of NVA. They carried large packs camouflaged with tree branches and walked on the same trail we had hammered in the morning. I again called for fire for effect with high-explosive rounds. This time the artillery battery got creative and walked six rounds right down the trail, covering about one hundred meters. Ayers could not believe his eyes. Trying not to show any emotion, he said, "Sir, those rounds just tore the hell out of that column of NVA. Sir, we're kicking their butts. Aruuu-uuugah!" Ayers had mounted the M-1 spotter scope on a tripod, so the piece was now trained on the trail and set in perfectly.

I dropped down next to Ayers, saying, "Let me see what the hell is going on out there." Although the trail was about three thousand meters across the valley, the power of the spotter scope brought the NVA up very clearly. I half whispered, as if we were close enough to the NVA for them to hear us, and said, "Unbelievable they are out there picking up their people and equipment, but they are still coming down that trail. Tell the artillery battery to fire for effect again; don't change anything. Tell them what they just did. This is unbelievable." Ayers ordered up the same artillery package, and I observed the impact. "Bingo," I whispered as the artillery rounds once again marched up the trail, vaporizing everything that was moving. I pulled my eyes away from the spotter scope and fixed them on Ayers.

Ayers smiled and said, "I know exactly what you are thinking, Lieutenant."

"Yeah, Sarge, we got to get into the Que Sons and find out what's going on up there. This scuttlebutt about Front Four being in the area may not be farfetched."

The next nine days, Ayers and I had hundreds of daily sightings of NVA using the trail coming out of the Que Son Mountains. They were bold and undaunted by our artillery fire. The major adjustment that they made in their movement was merely to spread their ranks. Sometimes they would send only one or two of their soldiers at a time along the open portion of the trail we could reach with our artillery fire. Of course, we were sure they were using the trail at night, so the artillery battery lobbed a few rounds out there just to try and keep them honest. At dusk, we saw the NVA moving on the trail, and at dawn, there was still movement. Whenever, I mercilessly continued the payback. The move from An Hoa to Hill 34 had created enough of a distraction in the rear that no one seemed to be paying much attention to our reports from the usually quiet OP. First Force, for all practical purposes, had stood down for training, and we were the only team left in the field. Simmons finally had time to study the reports of Hanover Sue's sighting and artillery missions. He waited eagerly for the team's return, because he had questions that he knew only I could really answer. It is strange in a war how significant bits of intelligence like that huge movement of enemy troops can almost be lost. Timing is everything in combat. Extremely important opportunities are sometimes lost when they are not recognized in time. But those sightings really did not fall through the cracks; they alerted Major Simmons to the possibility that something important was going on in the Que Son Mountains.

From the air, Hill 34 looked like a paradise compared to 1st Force's old home in the An Hoa basin. The compound was a couple of hundred meters long and about 150 meters wide. Its defensive positions were well built, with bunkers and wire laid out strategically around the entire perimeter. Tin-roofed and screened-in barracks were neatly lined up in the middle of the compound. Shade trees grew over some of the buildings. A large mess hall and enlisted man's bar could be seen just on the edge of the metal helo pad. The prop blast from our chopper blew a cloud of dust across the hill as we landed. Sergeant Ayers took charge of the team as soon as we landed and went looking for the platoon's new hootch. Major Simmons was standing on the helo pad, waiting patiently for me. I saluted him, and as he returned my salute, he joked, "Where have you been, Lieutenant Peters, on R and R?"

"No, sir, I've been up on the OP," I answered, as if he didn't know. I could tell he was anxious for the particulars on what I had seen.

"Let's go up to my office," he said. "I want to hear all about what you've seen."

"The major has an office? No more tents! This place is all right, sir," I remarked.

We ascended a half-dozen steps to the major's modest office, a well-built structure with a couple of exits, map-covered walls, and decent lighting. I got right to the point. "Sir, we have got to get into the Que Sons, because there are more NVA pouring in and out of there than you can believe." Pointing to a large wall map, Simmons asked me to show him the route the NVA were using. I drew the trail across the map. "Sir, the movement involves Antenna Valley and the Que Son Valley as well as the mountains. This movement is huge and bold." The major listened intently as I explained the route that I thought the NVA was using to move troops in and out of the Que Sons and into the valleys.

Not wanting to dampen my enthusiasm, Simmons hesitated, then spoke. "Listen, Lieutenant, we'll get into the Que Sons just as soon as we finish some training and one special mission on the Laotian border for Three MAF."

I frowned as I listened, then shot back in disbelief, "Sir, that won't be too late, will it?"

"I don't know, Lieutenant, sometimes these targets of opportunity come and go. But I've got a gut feeling that the NVA are moving into the Que Sons, not out of them. They are still going to be there in two weeks. Maybe they need to get comfortable."

The next morning, Simmons sent word to me that he wanted me to report to his office immediately. Captain Williams greeted me at the door to the major's office and ushered me in. Simmons got right to the point. "Lieutenant, your team is pretty beat up. You've lost an experienced point man, and a couple of your men are acting as if they have had too many patrols. How would you like some new men that you can train your way? You would be building a new team. Of course, you would keep Ayers because you two seem to work well together, but the rest of 2d Platoon would be transferred to other jobs in the company."

I answered immediately. "Sir, the lieutenant would really welcome the opportunity to train a new team. When could we get started?"

"We are starting our new training cycle tomorrow," he replied. He was not wasting any time as he handed me a new 2d Platoon roster along with an operation order for a mission requested by III MAF. Then he said, "You have two weeks to get this new team ready. So you better get out of here and get to work."

"Yes, sir," I answered. I did an about-face, exited the major's office, and headed for 2d Platoon's hootch in search of Sergeant Ayers.

Second Platoon's hootch was empty. A note was nailed to the door that simply stated, "We'll miss you, Mother," and was signed by 2d Platoon. Just about the time I murmured under my breath, "Where the hell is Ayers," I heard someone holler my name.

"Lieutenant Peters, sir." It was Ayers. I returned his salute. In a worried voice, Ayers began, "Sir, we got a problem. Our whole platoon has been transferred. Second Platoon's hootch is empty. All that's left is a note referring to me as Mother, which no one under the rank of sergeant ever gets away with calling me. What the hell happened?"

I laughed as I handed Ayers the new platoon roster. "Mother, I mean Sergeant, find these men," I said, smiling, "and move them into 2d Platoon's hootch. Have them in formation in front of my quarters at 1600 hours dressed in full 782 gear with their weapons."

"Yes, sir," Ayers responded. He saluted and sprinted off into the compound. He obviously had picked up on my enthusiasm and was now going to do his part to make it happen. "Sarge," I shouted.

"Yes, sir?"

"I'd get that note to Mother off 2d Platoon's hootch door before the new troops spot it."

"Yes, sir. I plan to do that right away," Ayers shouted back.

Promptly at 1600 hours, Ayers knocked on the officers' hootch hatchway. I slipped into my Ranger straps, adjusted my patrolling gear, and grabbed my new weapon of choice, a 9mm Swedish-K automatic rifle. The Swedish-K had a short barrel and a 36-round magazine, which made it handy in the bush and helpful in a firefight. It also had an open bolt, which kept it from bad jams. Ayers greeted me when I stepped from the hootch, growling, "Sir, 2d Platoon is ready for inspection."

"Let's see how they look," I replied. Ayers brought the platoon to attention. I began the inspection by saying, "When I get to you, I want you to give your name, rank, and what part of the country you are from." As I went

through the ranks of about fifteen men, I chose five men
for the first patrol. I was just using my instincts at that
point, but I knew that during the training I could change
personnel if I needed. My new point would be a short,
stocky private first class and former high-school football
player from Alabama named Wix. L. Cpl. Mike Foley, a
college dropout, had communications training, so I planned
to have him handle primary radio. Private First Class
Horn, a baby-faced kid from the Midwest, looked real
alert, so I figured I would turn him into a point man, too.
Private First Class Adams, a big, tough-looking kid from
California's Mojave Desert, would run deuce point. Private Meinheit would handle the secondary radio. A trained
corpsman named Thomas would become our platoon doc.
With Ayers running tail-end Charlie and myself walking
third man, we would have a seven-man team ready for the
mission. The rest of the new men would only be a supporting cast while I worked hard with those seven men.

The next two weeks of training were extremely intense,
even by Force Recon standards. From dusk to dawn 2d
Platoon trained, learning hand signals, how to let their
weapons follow their eyes, how to open C ration cans and
eat quietly, how to break an ambush. From a hovering
CH-46 helicopter, they learned how to rappel into the
jungle. I took them into thick vegetation in a training area
near the China Beach R & R center to work on patrolling
techniques.

We practiced walking down sixty-foot-long cable ladders that hung off the skids on both sides of an army Huey
helicopter. The men had to walk down the ladders in perfect timing, one man on one side of the chopper and another man on the opposite side. It was a swinging trapeze

act that could bring the Huey down if it was not done properly.

With the help of skilled pilots and the CH-46 helicopter, we learned how to be extracted from the jungle on the SPIE rig. The SPIE rig was introduced by Major Simmons during the early part of our training. The major's invention was received by his recon Marines with a lot of enthusiasm because it added a whole new dimension to 1st Force's growing arsenal of equipment. The rig was specifically designed to rescue teams from the mountainous Central Highlands through any small break in the thick jungle canopy. The CH-46 helicopter, with the rig attached to its hellhole, could pick up a recon team like a bunch of puppets. Then the team could be flown home, dangling from the bottom of the chopper at an altitude of about three thousand feet.

The missions that 1st Force was being asked to run for III MAF were exotic and extremely long range. My team's mission was to monitor a busy spur of the Ho Chi Minh trail right on the Laotian border, forty-four miles southwest of Da Nang. Our secondary mission was to search for a possible prisoner-of-war camp in the area. Wayne Rollings had been selected for a mission to search for and locate a suspected enemy tank park located in his patrolling area. Sergeant Theodore Ott also pulled a mission to search for an NVA regimental communications center. The terrain where these missions were to be run was covered by two-hundred-foot triple jungle canopy, the likes of which few Americans had yet set foot under. The missions called for the deepest reconnaissance the Marine Corps ever attempted during the Vietnam War, but they were delayed for three days because the air wing package to support missions of that magnitude did not yet exist.

The night before the mission, the helo pad on Hill 34 looked like a helicopter show. There were four CH-46s, four Cobra gunships, four Huey gunships, and two Huey slicks. Rollings and I compared notes that night as we stood next to all the hardware. Rollings was philosophical. "Paco, this is the kind of mission that Force Recon is supposed to be running. Damn, we're going out forty-four miles on this one. That's a long way to have to walk home."

Without taking my eyes off the helicopters, I answered, "Yeah, there are lots of bad guys between here and there. Lots of mountain ranges and rivers to cross. I'm glad we've got a ride out there and a ride home."

Rollings and I had drawn a couple of dream missions. What remained to be seen was if III MAF would be able to support three teams simultaneously so deep in enemy-controlled territory. This was one of those no-guts, no-glory moments.

One hour before first light, Hill 34 came alive as the Cobra helicopters, one by one, lifted up off the steel pad and disappeared into the darkness. The Huey gunships were next as they rose up and chased after the Cobras. The entire 1st Force compound vibrated as those magnificent aircraft broke the predawn silence. The tin-roofed hootches rattled, and their screened-in sides sagged from the violent prop blast that caused a strong wind to blow across the hill.

Three perfectly equipped and camouflaged Force Recon teams stood at the north end of the landing zone. I stood at the front of my six-man team, Hanover Sue, which upon command boarded one of the two army Huey slicks, which were piloted by warrant officers. The team had to climb over rolled-up four-foot-wide, sixty-foot-long cable ladders hanging from the skids on both sides of the chopper.

Ayers counted the team and gave me a thumbs-up. I, in turn, gave the Huey's crew chief the thumbs-up. The young army warrant officer pilot's call sign was Rattle Snake Two-eight. We had barely lifted off the pad when they gunned their engines and, with the nose of the bird down, drove their craft like a race car at low level. Within seconds, they had swung the Hueys west in the direction of Laos. Rollings's eight-man team, Lunch Meat, boarded one CH-46 while Sergeant Ott's team, Golden State, jogged onto a second 46. Within seconds, the teams were in the air, also headed west toward the Laotian Border. Lunch Meat's and Golden State's inserts went well. There was no prepping of the LZs with air strikes, a standard operations procedure that had finally been overturned at the III MAF level. The 46s showed up at dawn, dropped the teams, and left before anyone could see them. Rollings's and Ott's teams were inserted without incident into a very heavily defended NVA base-camp area. The element of surprise and the fact of American presence that deep in enemy-controlled territory was something new.

Hanover Sue's Hueys arrived on schedule over an LZ that was halfway up the side of a huge mountain. The crew chief cut the ties holding the ladders, and when the ladders completely unrolled, they touched the ground perfectly, sixty feet beneath the chopper. Ayers from one side of the chopper and Private First Class Wix, the point man, on the other side, descended the ladders. Next, the primary radioman and I started down the ladders in unison, but without warning, the radioman went into a thirty-foot free fall, landing on Private First Class Wix and momentarily knocking him unconscious. The warrant officer pilot performed every maneuver possible to keep his chopper from crashing because of the sudden shift of weight, and swaying wildly I hung beneath the Huey until the pilot steadied the craft. Then I continued down the last thirty feet of ladder to the ground. My last two men, a corpsman and a secondary radioman, came down the ladder quickly and joined the team on the ground.

I quickly assessed the situation. The primary radioman could not move because of back and rib injuries, and the point man was dazed. I needed at least five men to continue the mission, so I kept the point man with the team. Within minutes, a 46 was lowering a medevac basket to Hanover Sue. The corpsman tended to the wounded Marine until he was lifted up in the basket to the hovering medevac chopper. My team had already drawn too much attention, and the mission had probably been compromised during the medevac. Ayers and I huddled up for a minute and whispered quietly about where to go from here. I said, "Let's not use this ridgeline to climb up the mountain. I've got a bad feeling about that direction."

Nodding his head, Ayers pointed to a deep, densely foliated draw just below us. "Nobody will ever find us in there. We can crawl to the bottom and start up that ridgeline over there," he whispered.

I grinned, rolled my eyes, and said, "Let's move out."

Just as Hanover Sue disappeared into the draw, and while Ayers was carefully disguising our entry point, over thirty NVA ran down the ridge looking for us. Ayers told me later he froze as he peeked through the vines he had woven together to cover the team's trail. All he could see run past at his eye level were NVA boots and Ho Chi Minh sandals. He heard the familiar rattle of the slings knocking against the wooden stocks of the AK-47 assault rifles. After the last of the unit had passed, Ayers inched his way through the tunnel that Hanover Sue had made as we crawled on our hands and knees under the lush foliage. Even Ayers, the master tail-end Charlie, did not attempt to cover up the entire tunnel. It could not be detected from the ridgeline because of the dense vegetation, so he merely disguised the entrance for a few meters, then followed the rest of the team. I had taken point and was painstakingly cutting a path through the undergrowth.

Hanover Sue's movement was slow, only fifty feet or so an hour. At that rate, the team would not reach its objective on the other side of the mountain range for at least three days. The mission was off to a horrible start, and I was deeply concerned. Finally, just before dark, I quietly cut through the last of the undergrowth and stood up at the base of a huge hardwood tree standing at least two hundred feet tall. The root system stuck out of the ground, long arteries rising as high as three feet in some places. I motioned to Ayers as the wily old sergeant came out of the tunnel smiling.

"That was a real adventure, Lieutenant," he growled.

"We'll harbor up here for the night," I whispered, pointing to the base of the tree.

I ordered Ayers to check out the heavily wooded ridgeline above us. It was too quiet. No birds were singing, and the closer he got to the top of the mountain, the more danger he felt. He stopped, took a knee, and just listened until it was dusk. There wasn't a sound coming off the mountain, and that probably meant the NVA knew a recon team was somewhere in the area and they had ambushes set to destroy it. The NVA had probably stopped their normal duties and gone on full alert. We were in big trouble. Ayers returned to the team at last light and shared his concerns with me. To compound the team's problems, my point man, Wix, was showing signs of a concussion. I couldn't trust him to take point. That left only four healthy team members to pull off the mission.

Ayers barely slept the entire night. Rather than passing the radio watch on, he stood it himself, allowing the team to sleep. I needed the rest after having to cut the team through some of the worst terrain I'd encountered in Vietnam. When there was enough light to see each other's eyes, Ayers and I exchanged signs that indicated we both sensed the danger. We gently awoke the team, signaling the slicing motion to our throats with our index finger that meant do not move. We sat motionless from 0600 until 0900 hours. Finally, the decision of whether or not to move was made for us. Ayers signaled me that I needed to take a radio transmission and gently passed the receiver to me. As I pressed the receiver to my ear, I heard Major Simmons, ordering us not to move because Lunch Meat and Golden State were both in heavy contact with NVA, and he could not guarantee us timely air support if we made contact.

Upon Simmons's request I shared the condition of my team. He was uneasy about Hanover Sue's continuing the mission. The major knew that six healthy Marines would have trouble getting the job done; the odds were not good with only four able to fight. Simmons's final words were "Hanover Sue, hold your position and under no circumstances initiate contact with the enemy."

I began to monitor Rollings's and Ott's contacts with the NVA. Golden State was in the worst trouble. The entire seven-man team had been shot up in a violent firefight with a tough NVA unit. Their point man, Private First Class Murphy, was holding off the NVA so that the team could escape. Sergeant Ott, the team leader, had taken three AK-47 rounds in the stomach but was continuing to lead the patrol. The rest of the team all had enemy bullets in them and were carrying and pulling one another to safety. Then Murphy's body jerked violently and fell to the ground. With Murphy out of the picture, the NVA used classic fire and maneuver tactics to work their way to the main body of the patrol. But the sight of Murphy lying in the open stirred the enraged Marines to counterattack and recover his lifeless body. Through willpower alone, Ott managed to remain conscious. Then the team was being safely pulled out of the jungle on the SPIE rig and headed back to Hill 34.

Once Golden State was successfully extracted, I switched to Lunch Meat's radio frequency. I learned that Rollings had found a thick communications line and had followed it to the outskirts of what he thought was a tank park and fuel depot. But the NVA were forcing him back to his insert zone. They obviously did not want a recon team nosing around or getting into a firefight around the fuel. So, after a brief firefight, the NVA had Lunch Meat surrounded and were forcing the team back to where the team could be extracted. First Force was dealing with the best soldiers and support groups the North Vietnamese had to offer. The smart, sophisticated fighters were trying to guide Rollings's team to a safe extract zone, so they whistled and made noise to let Lunch Meat know not to go this way or that way, channeling the team straight to its original landing zone. Of course, Rollings wasn't buying that, not for a minute; the seasoned Marine was pinpointing the target on his map and ordering up a massive air strike on the suspected fuel depot even as he allowed the NVA to usher him out of the area. That Georgia farm boy was nobody's fool. He had smelled the fuel and heard the tractorlike engine of a tank briefly start and then shut down. The NVA were in for a big surprise when Lunch Meat got pulled out.

The big CH-46 arrived on schedule just as Lunch Meat reached its extract LZ. They were left unchallenged by the NVA. Quickly the team was in the air and circling to gain altitude. Rollings's head and shoulders hung out of one of the circular windows of the 46. He squinted to get the best look he could at the imminent explosion on the jungle floor below. He smirked when the first Phantom made its pass over the target. As the sleek bomber dropped its load of five-hundred-pound bombs and napalm, an orange ball of fire rose several hundred feet into the air. Then black smoke with orange secondary explosions broke through the thick green jungle canopy. Lunch Meat let out a loud cheer as Rollings hung out of the chopper window with a fist raised in defiance of the enemy he had just destroyed.

The distant air strikes and helicopter activity were the only sounds that had broken the eerie silence hanging over Hanover Sue's position. I motioned Ayers to join me for a situation report. Ayers climbed over the thick roots and sat down next to me. Not wanting the rest of the team to know that Garden State had taken heavy casualties, I whispered the details directly into Ayers's ear. Our conversation was interrupted when Simmons summoned me to the radio. Hanover Sue was going to have to go out by ladder, because the SPIE rig had been shot on Ott's extract and was deemed unsafe. Of course, because of the height of the trees on the steep ridgeline, the ladder would barely reach us. Through hand signals, Ayers passed the word to prepare for a ladder extract. Within the hour, a CH-46 was hovering at treetop level above our position. The ladder was dropped but it missed reaching us by about twenty feet, swaying far above our outstretched hands. Then automatic fire exploded from scores of weapons on top of the mountain and the crew chief in the 46 clutched his thighs as bullets sank deep into his flesh. Rounds shattered the Plexiglas around the cockpit, and the ladder momentarily tangled in the trees as the pilot tried to gain control of the bird and pull away from the side of the mountain. With a burst of power, the chopper freed itself, tearing off a ten-foot section of the metal rungs. Only the skill of a veteran pilot like Maj. Owen C. "Mad Dog" Baker could have kept the chopper from crashing into the jungle. Even so, his engines were struggling to produce the power he needed, so the major headed for the valley floor before finally gaining full control. Then he turned the damaged 46 eastward toward Da Nang as aviation fuel dripped from its ruptured tanks.

Our instincts had been correct. The enemy had just been waiting for the recon team to surface. Now that they had a better idea of Hanover Sue's location, they would be coming for us. I quickly grabbed the radio handset and ordered air strikes to be run all the way around our position. I was sealing off all access routes to the ridgeline that we occupied. Within a couple of minutes, an aerial observer was putting the air strikes anywhere I felt I needed them. Because of the volume of fire taken by Major Baker's chopper, the wing decided to try overkill on the mountain by running two hours of air strikes. That devastated the NVA, whose resistance remained strong for only the first hour. Nevertheless, helicopters still could not get close to our position until finally all ground-to-air fire ceased.

Once again Simmons's voice came up over the radio, this time to say, "Hanover Sue, get ready for a SPIE rig extract. Be advised: if we don't get you this time, you will be spending the night."

Within a beat, I responded, saying, "This is Hanover Sue Six, I copy that King Fish will come and get us." Simmons *had* to be somewhere above our position in a command bird or he would not have been able to communicate so clearly with me. I also felt that if the action went into the night, the team would be overrun and wiped out. The one chance to get off that mountain was Simmons's SPIE rig. But there were several variables that weighed heavily on Simmons. One was the fact that the rig had a bullet hole in it. The major was also betting his career by using the SPIE rig at all, because it had not yet been officially sanctioned for Marine Corps use. Then, to compound the problems, his command chopper got hit with ground fire, wounding him in the eye.

We barely had time to prepare the harnesses and nylon ropes when suddenly all hell broke loose. Phantoms were making low passes over the mountain, firing cannons and rockets. Cobras and Hueys were doing the same. The OV-10 spotter plane was even getting into the act by diving toward the mountain and firing rockets. In the midst of that awesome display of airpower, one lone CH-46 arrived at treetop level and dropped the SPIE rig through a large hole in the canopy. It reached us with just ten feet to spare. Within thirty seconds, I was hollering over the radio to the pilot, "Go, go, go." The 46 pulled the team straight up through the trees with such power that when we cleared the canopy, we were stretched out parallel to the jungle ceiling beneath us. Whoever was flying the extract chopper was not taking any chances of getting stuck in the trees. If we cleared the canopy without losing our heads, arms, or legs, I knew we would be okay. Any brush with a tree limb at the speed of our extract would have meant sudden death.

Off the side of the mountain, the team flew suspended on the rig beneath the chopper. At dusk, against the backdrop of an orange sunset, Hanover Sue flew over mountains and rivers. You could not get a better view of Vietnam's countryside. Everything looked green and lush from three thousand feet. It was so cool and quiet at that altitude. You can't buy a ride like this anywhere, I thought. It was spectacular, and way down deep, I knew the rescue was another miracle. I wanted to believe that someone in heaven was looking after Hanover Sue.

The long ride home left the men's legs numb from the lack of proper circulation. When we hit the helo pad on Hill 34, we could barely walk. I picked myself up off the hard metal and quickly counted my team members one more time. I had made the count coming off the mountain, but it had been a long ride. I walked a few steps, and there were Major Simmons and Captain Williams with big grins. Without mentioning what Hanover Sue had just been through, Simmons looked me in the eye and said, "Well, Lieutenant, are you ready to go into the Que Sons?"

During 1st Force's foray into the Laotian border NVA base camps, a few thousand miles away on Midway Island, two powerful men, one American and the other Vietnamese, strolled along the ocean. The two men were both presidents of their nations. They stopped to talk on a beautiful bluff overlooking the rugged coastline. At nearly the same time in Da Nang, Private First Class Murphy's lifeless body was being loaded onto a transport plane headed to Dover Air Force Base. The Vietnamese man was South Vietnam's President Thieu. The American was President Nixon. Against the backdrop of the blue Pacific Ocean,

Nixon was laying down the law to Thieu. Nixon, without blinking, told Thieu that the United States would withdraw twenty-five thousand of its troops by the end of August. Thieu considered "withdrawal" a defeatist term and probably would have preferred some phrase like "replacement of American troops."

Thieu, who was barely holding together a handful of factions in South Vietnam, knew that America's decision to withdraw, if it was interpreted as such, would further divide his weak coalition. He had struggled mightily to unite the National Democratic Social Front, the Social Humanist Party, the Revolutionary Dai Viet, and the Social Democratic Party to defeat the Communist's political as well as their military advances.

The decision had been made between Nixon and a man named Henry A. Kissinger, who Thieu did not even know existed. Kissinger, a Harvard professor, was now serving as Nixon's new assistant for national security affairs. In the preceding months, he and his staff had been forcing the army, the State Department, and others to analyze their positions afresh on the subject of Vietnam.

In his own mind, Nixon's return to the United States from Midway Island was one of great triumph. On June 17, 1969, Air Force One touched down at Andrews Air Force Base a few hours after Private First Class Murphy's flag-draped casket was carried into one of Dover Air Force Base's abandoned hangars.

Within hours, Nixon and Kissinger were standing live before a national television audience announcing their plan to Vietnamize the war. Nixon, with total resolve, said, "We hope to withdraw 100,000 troops by the end of 1969, and up to 150,000 in 1970."

Almost simultaneously in Paris, Senator George Mc-

Govern, after meeting secretly with the chief North Vietnamese negotiator, stepped before a jungle of news microphones and cameras at the Majestic Hotel. He dropped a bombshell when he stated emphatically, "Fruitful negotiations cannot begin until the United States agrees to unconditional withdrawal and ultimately discontinues its unqualified embrace of the South Vietnamese government." Henry Cabot Lodge, the president's officially appointed negotiator at the Paris peace talks, sat in his room at the Majestic Hotel, enraged by McGovern's undermining of the United States' position. He had spent months working toward a timed mutual withdrawal of both American and North Vietnamese troops from South Vietnam.

Meanwhile, in a message to President Thieu that was made public, Bui Diem, the South Vietnamese ambassador to the United States, characterized the U.S. policy of negotiation as a withdrawal. In a press interview held in his embassy office, Diem stated emphatically, "The die has been cast, and America, in my view, is beginning the abandonment of South Vietnam."

A half a world away, North Vietnam's aging president, Ho Chi Minh, was caught on camera by an international French news agency urging the Vietnamese, "Fight until the United States is defeated and leaves Vietnam."

Within a couple of days, all of this political information had probably reached the North Vietnamese Army's Front Four command group in the jungles of the Central Highlands of South Vietnam. I am sure they were encouraged that their efforts to launch a summer offensive were not in vain. I could picture them huddled together in a cave deep in the heart of the Que Son Mountains mapping out every detail of the offensive. We didn't know it then, but NVA counterreconnaissance teams were assigned by Front

Four to seek out and hunt down all Force Recon teams trying to run patrols in the Central Highlands from the Que Sons to the Laotian border.

CHAPTER 9

The Fourth of July

First Force's new home on Hill 34 was a peaceful setting in comparison to the one at An Hoa. The compound had been built by an engineer battalion and provided the best in living conditions. For the officers and men of 1st Force Recon, accustomed to spartan conditions at An Hoa, the hill with its mature shade trees, mess halls, officer and enlisted clubs, was more like an R & R center than a permanent base of operation. Gone were the tents, the noisy artillery battery, the mud and the dust of the An Hoa basin. The troops lived in screened, tin-roofed hootches whose plywood floors were built up off the ground to keep water out. A friendly village with beautifully cared for rice paddies wrapped itself around the base of the hill just outside the defensive wire. On Hill 34, the biggest danger to 1st Force was complacency. The atmosphere could become too comfortable for a unit that had to perform at a very high level of proficiency or die.

Rollings and I sat in the officers' hootch sipping a beer and comparing notes on our Laotian border patrols. We had not showered yet, so our faces were still a mixture of green camouflage greasepaint and sweat. We looked rough, but we didn't care; that day we had been through the fire. We were speaking candidly about everything we had been doing since we reported to 1st Force, asking the hard questions about the effectiveness of the patrols. We had risked our lives and the lives of our men, and in doing so, we really knew that the enemy threat was much greater than what Henry Kissinger could ever dream.

Speaking in a low voice, as though I were still on patrol, I said, "We don't need to go to the Laotian border for the kind of action we had today. I spotted hundreds of NVA pouring out of the Que Sons just three weeks ago. I was up on the OP, and you wouldn't believe what I saw—"

Rollings cut me off. "Paco, I believe you. My last patrol near the Que Sons, you remember, was when Ritchie's chopper went down and we had to scratch that mission and all."

I nodded, saying, "Yeah, sure, what happened?"

"Well, I got on the edge of the Que Sons a few days later, and the weather turned real bad, and we couldn't get any air support. I was being real careful and movin' real slow with the team when we found this NVA base camp. It was under some triple canopy, and the trees were at least three hundred feet tall. There was no way you could see this from the air. It looked like it had not been touched by any air strikes or artillery. There were women walking around, and I mean beautiful Vietnamese women. An NVA couple came running through the jungle and made love within ten meters of our position. There was something about this NVA unit that was different. These were high-ranking dudes, if you know what I mean. The honcho of this outfit had a thatched-roof hootch of his own. I watched it for two days. Every day, this beautiful woman would visit this honcho's hootch and spend several hours alone with him. I don't think they were talking about the war. I was dying to blow this place away, but the weather was so bad nothing was flying. The artillery battery from An Hoa couldn't touch this place, because it was on the reverse side of the mountains. Then, right before the weather broke, the unit moved out of the camp. There they all were, in a long column with all their communications gear. It looked like an antenna farm with all the aerials. Rolls of communications wire were slung over these troops' shoulders. There was an elite security unit around the honcho. These guys had high-and-tight haircuts. Some wore side arms. All of them had AK-47s outfitted with jungle slings. They walked in groups of twos and fives. I got a good look at these dudes. They were really hard core."

I listened intently to Rollings's story. Until then, none of the patrols seemed to have any connection to each other. The missions were not lacking action, but they seemed to lack focus. First Force was generating an overwhelming number of sightings and contacts with the NVA. It seemed as if the 1st Marine Division, III Marine Amphibious Force, and MACV, the top command over the war, were all having trouble processing the mountain of intelligence.

I started putting things together in my own mind. The base camp that Rick and I had spent the five days in was not the head of the monster. It was just part of the trail network and overnight quarters for the NVA's movement into the Central Highlands. All the sightings and firefights that 1st Force had those past few months had been more of the random stuff that didn't go anywhere. What Rollings had run into, with the women and senior NVA officers, was more a part of the head of the monster. The real danger to the stability of Da Nang and the rest of Quang Nam Province was not out on the Laotian border. It was much closer than that. Maybe as close as the Que Son Mountains. The mountains were right in the middle of the province and only a two-day walk from Da Nang.

My thoughts were rudely interrupted as Champe, Ritchie, and Miller burst into the hootch. They were all in fresh jungle utilities, clean shaven, and showered. They had gold parachute wings all shined up and pinned above their hearts on their camouflaged blouses. "Come on, Paco, get your ass cleaned up; we are going to party tonight, bro," Lowder shouted with a Latino accent.

"Oh yeah, where we going?" I asked cautiously.

"We're going up to Battalion Recon on Hill 327, Paco, for the change-of-command dinner, bro," Miller chimed in. "Come on, Rollings! Get squared away, bro, it's party time," Champe growled. Within thirty minutes, we were all in the back of a PC truck headed on the paved road that snaked its way up Hill 327, which was also the home of the 1st Marine Division headquarters. Gen. Ormond R. Simpson was the commanding general of the division. We didn't see much of him, because we had been working for III MAF, his superiors, for the past few months. General Simpson had a gift for remembering the hundreds of names of the officers under his command. Sure enough, when we entered the Battalion Recon officers club, there stood General Simpson with his hand extended to his Force Recon officers. He reeled off each one of our names as he shook our hand and welcomed us to the party. And what a party it was. Steak and lobster was the main course. We ate and drank until we couldn't stand up. Our lieutenant buddies from Battalion Recon, guys like Jack Holly, Chip Gregson, and Willie Oller, made us feel real welcome. Another lieutenant, Steve "Sugar Bear" Corbette, was also present on this unforgettable evening. Sugar Bear was temporarily on loan to 1st Force from Battalion Recon and would show up like a recurring character in a TV series. He was a real hell-raiser and an excellent recon Marine.

We were raising hell at our table, which was located right in front of the entertainment. A Philippine floor show was trying to make us feel at home by playing popular American rock music. The louder the music got, the rowdier the lieutenants' table got. We were all gunfighters—bush recon Marines—so the senior officers just stood around the edge of the club and let us enjoy ourselves. By that time in June, 1st Force Recon had more sightings and kills than the entire 1st Marine Division; we deserved a little liberty, and believe me, we were taking it. The evening came to a sudden end when Sugar Bear dared Miller to dance with the lead singer of the band, a pretty little thing. Unfortunately, he stumbled up to her, knocking her into the drums, which came crashing down on the floor with her in the middle of them. That was it; a major led us out to our truck and told us to go home.

The next morning, Champe and Ritchie headed for scuba school in the Philippines. Miller headed for thirty days' leave back to the United States. I looked around the empty officers' hootch and motioned to Rollings, saying, "Man, it's like a ghost town around here without the rest of the bros. I hear you're going to jump school, too."

Rollings, looking a little guilty, replied, "Yeah, I'll be joining Lowder on Okinawa in two days." I looked around the hootch again, realizing that I was the only operational lieutenant left for probably the next month. The weight of the responsibility fell on me like a ten-ton gorilla. It was going to be strange without the other lieutenants. We had become one another's strength. I knew that real soon I was headed into the Que Sons, and it was no mystery to me what awaited my team in those haunted mountains.

The next morning, there was an excitement in my soul as I walked across the compound. This was a new day. An Hoa and the experience I had gathered in the field the past few months was about to begin to pay off. I glanced at the operation order that Major Simmons had just handed me a few minutes earlier. I quickly unbuttoned the lower pocket on my jungle utilities, pulled out my map, and checked the grid square for the patrol. Much to my disappointment, it was nowhere near the Que Sons.

My team had drawn a pathfinder mission. We were to be dropped into the jungle a couple of miles from an abandoned fire support base south of An Hoa. There, in three days, we were to link up with another team at the base and secure landing zones for the insert of a thousand-man infantry battalion—not an American battalion, a South Vietnamese Army battalion. The first fruits of Washington, D.C.'s Vietnamization program was about to begin officially.

My first thought was that I hoped the Vietnamese would be briefed that two American Force Recon teams were securing the LZ. I didn't want them opening fire on us as they exited their choppers. The mission was real tricky. Two teams, dropped six miles apart, would have to weave their way through the very numerous enemy and the jungle and meet, at night, in a clearing on top of a mountain with a fire-support base (FSB). The NVA loved to hang out around these abandoned forts and shoot down any choppers trying to land troops in the area. After Ric Miller and I had almost bought the farm on old FSB Cutlass, we made a deal with the wing that Force Recon would lay off inserts into those places.

Later that day, Rollings informed me that his platoon sergeant, E-5 Mormon, would be leading the other team assigned to the pathfinder mission. Rollings spoke highly of Mormon, who was relatively new to the company. When I asked where I could find him to discuss the mission, Rollings pointed at a figure who was exiting the compound's front gate about a hundred meters away. Mormon stripped to the waist and, wearing tiger-stripe shorts and jungle boots with a rifle strapped across his back, disappeared out the gate on a dead run. "Where in the hell is he going in such a hurry?" I asked.

"Oh, Mormon, he's adopted some kids at an orphanage about eight miles from here, and he is taking some money to them," Rollings replied.

"He's running eight miles to an orphanage? How is he getting back?"

"He's gonna run back," Rollings replied.

I was impressed. "When can I meet with this guy about the mission?"

"He's got the perimeter duty tonight. Why don't you look him up then," Rollings offered.

It was pitch black on Hill 34 that night as I went looking for Sergeant Mormon. A few lights beaming from the hootches in the village outside our defensive wire helped me in my search. I got to a bunker where I could barely discern a flashlight flickering from inside. I made out the silhouette of a Marine manning an M-60 machine gun while peering out into the night. From inside the bunker, I could hear a voice reading a familiar verse from the Bible. Then I heard a young Marine's voice say, "What does that mean, Sergeant Mormon?"

With real authority in his voice, Mormon began patiently answering his question. I stood there as if frozen. What was I getting into on this pathfinder mission? Who is this guy who runs to orphanages and teaches the Bible to the troops? Suddenly Sergeant Mormon stepped from the bunker, quickly saluted me, and said, "Good evening, Lieutenant Peters."

I returned the salute and the greeting. Then I couldn't contain myself. "Sergeant Mormon, what is it about you? I saw you this morning running out the gate to visit an orphanage, and now here you are reading the Bible to the troops. There is something different about you. What is it? Are you religious or something?"

He came to attention, and with our faces just a few inches apart, he looked me straight in the eye and said, "Sir, I accepted Jesus Christ as my personal savior when I joined the Marine Corps."

My mouth must have fallen open. I thought, How could this guy believe that and do the kind of work we are called to do in Force Recon?

It was as if he read my mind. Without blinking, he added, "I know what you are thinking, Lieutenant; just know this, it all works out okay."

With those words came that same inner assurance and warmth that had swept over me when the chaplain at Quantico told me, "Lieutenant, go to Vietnam and lead men, because God has something for you there." I gathered myself quickly in front of Sergeant Mormon and got down to the business of planning the pathfinder mission. Something spiritual had been delivered to me that night, but we never spoke about it again.

Mormon, Ayers, and I rehearsed our teams for the task ahead of us. At dawn on the day of the mission, Mormon and I stood next to each other, ready to move our teams onto the choppers. Our faces were once again within inches of each other so that we could communicate in competition with the noise of the aircraft. "See you in three days on the mountain, Lieutenant," Mormon promised.

"Yeah, Sergeant, I'll be there."

For three days, Ayers and I worked feverishly, avoiding contact with the enemy. It took us a full day to move around an old bombed-out French château and estate that stood between us and our objective. The NVA were in abundance, which would be good training for the green South Vietnamese Army battalion. If we could get them safely on the ground, then they could slug it out with the bad guys we were dodging.

On the night of day three, I switched my radio frequency to a predesignated channel and began to whisper my position to Mormon, who was leading his team up the dark mountain. I'm sure we were both praying that the NVA hadn't slipped between us in the dark. Our silently finding each other in the dark and linking up our teams was going to be a long shot. All the junk we had learned Stateside about compass heading and night linkups was strictly for peacetime. We were in enemy-controlled territory, and reading a compass perfectly in the dark for several hundred meters isn't simple. Radio handsets pressed to our ears, Mormon and I had each taken point on our teams. Whispering and keying the handset were our only communication. Finally, each of us agreed to drop off the net and just use clicking sounds with our tongues. Within about ten steps' worth of tongue signals, Mormon's and my eyes met, our noses just inches apart. I recognized those eyes immediately. I counted our joining up as skill and luck that night. Today, I know it was simply a miracle. Mormon probably would agree.

At dawn, we laid out air panels for six LZs on the old fire support base. We owned the top of the mountain. With the rising sun of early morning as a backdrop, miles to the east, we suddenly could see and hear waves of CH-46 troop transport helicopters approaching our mountain six abreast. What a sight it was as those big birds stormed our position. After the ARVN had double-timed from their CH-46s, Mormon and I signaled our teams to board an outbound chopper. Our mission was successfully completed. We touched down at An Hoa, where an American general and a Vietnamese general came out on the metal runway and congratulated us for getting the battalion on the ground without a shot being fired. I've always felt that if they had prepped the fire support base with artillery or air strikes, the NVA in the area would have been waiting for them with .50-caliber antiaircraft fire for sure.

When I returned to Hill 34, I found out that Rollings hadn't left yet for jump school, so we had lunch together in the new officers' mess hall and laughed about the first lunch we had together at An Hoa. The lieutenants had never again eaten at the artillery battery after the rocket attack had blown the mess hall away; it was a cursed place in our minds. Rollings and I agreed that the lieutenants had been able to talk more openly and be themselves eating together in the tent at An Hoa. Concerning An Hoa, the lieutenants had a simple slogan: "An Hoa was all right." Although it was real tough out there for a few months, none of us would have traded the experience for anything.

When the mail arrived that afternoon, I was ready for some news from home. Pam's letter talked about San Francisco State and all the problems it was having. She said that S. I. Hayakawa, a world-class semanticist, had become president of the college. In one stroke of genius, he reduced the student activity fee from ten dollars a semester to one dollar. That dried up the student treasury so that the professional hell-raisers had to go to work someplace other than the campus. "No time to riot when you have to work for a living," Hayakawa stated. To me, what had been so important a year earlier paled in contrast to what was going on in my life in 1969. The revolution at San Francisco State was really kids' stuff. If some of the leaders of the revolution on campus really believed in their cause, then why were they quitting? I had not quit. As a matter of fact, I was risking my life to prove my convictions. Maybe it was all about money with these revolutionaries after all, I thought to myself.

One thing I did know for sure was that I was not trying to prove anything to anybody but myself anymore. Who the hell would ever believe what I was seeing in Vietnam anyway? My tour of duty was strictly for me. I dreamed about writing a book about this war. After all, I had a front-row seat at the cultural revolution of the sixties in San Francisco, and I was in a front-row seat in Vietnam. That's about as good as it gets for the 1960s, I reasoned.

A day after Rollings left for jump school, I boarded a chopper and headed into the Que Son Mountains, feeling real good about my new team because of our successful pathfinder mission. We were inserted at about 1400 hours on a hot July afternoon. As an experiment, I had the pilots insert the team on the reverse side of the Que Son mountain range from where I would actually run the patrol. I then had the team climb to the top of the mountain and walk along the narrow ridgeline. It was a great tactic, and we reached our objective without being detected. We were patrolling without the NVA suspecting that an American recon team was in the area.

I alternated between point and deuce point, teaching Wix and Horn how to handle both positions. Adams watched everything I was teaching the point men and seemed to be picking up his job as deuce point very quickly. This was nerve-racking on-the-job training. I worked hard with Wix and Horn while Ayers worked with Meinheit and Foley on the radios. Doc Thomas, the corpsman, moved very well with the team. The eight-man patrol moved without incident until late in the afternoon on the first day. After discovering an enemy hospital complex carved into the side of the mountain, we formed a defensive perimeter. I posted

Adams and Meinheit at the entrance. Ayers and I proceeded into the enemy installation, inspecting the little rooms and adjoining caves. Suddenly we heard automatic-weapon fire coming from the entrance.

Ayers and I sprinted back to the main body of the team. Once into the daylight at the mouth of the complex, we spotted Adams standing over the body of a dead NVA. Ayers had the team tighten the perimeter and get ready for action. Wix and I searched the enemy soldier, finding papers that would later prove he was from the 2d NVA Division, a huge enemy unit moving into the area. Then, using hand signals, I ordered the team to move out of the area, cautiously but quickly. The key was not to allow the enemy to see the team or to have any idea of its size. As long as the enemy did not see us, it would be pure speculation as to what kind of a unit had killed the NVA soldier. Escaping undetected now meant that we could continue the mission. A heavy rain began to fall, which helped cover any noise we made as we headed higher into the mountains.

Ayers did a masterful job making sure that the team was not followed while I took point and led them to higher ground. The idea was to put as much distance as possible between the point of contact and our harbor site. We had to do that before we were discovered or ran out of daylight. At that point, we were moving away from our objective. Ayers recognized what I was doing. We were leaving the area the same way that we had come into it. The team had not encountered the enemy in the direction that they were retreating. But to quickly move into an unknown area could mean disaster. The team would reenter the objective area in a day or two when things returned to normal. When I felt the team was far enough back up the mountain, I stopped and waited for Ayers. The contact had been a good learning situation for the new team. It had broken the ice.

Before leaving on that patrol, I reminded the team that individuals would be fined for coughing, snoring, or breaking noise discipline through carelessness. When Meinheit coughed while setting up the harbor site, I grabbed him by the throat and whispered, "That cough just cost you five bucks." There was no time to baby those young men; stupidity would get them killed real quick in the Que Sons. The rain had temporarily broken the oppressive heat and humidity of the jungle. There was a freshness in the air. Beads of water ran off the shiny leaves of the jungle's lush vegetation. A refreshing breeze began to blow across the mountain.

In the late-afternoon light, I squinted at my map, trying to plot a new route to our objective, an old French road connecting Antenna Valley on the east side of the Que Son Mountains with the Que Son Valley to the west. The new route I plotted on the map would cost the team another day, but the chance contact at the hospital complex could not have been avoided. Adams had done the right thing by quickly shooting the NVA soldier. If the man had escaped, our mission would have been compromised. When Ayers joined the team in the harbor site, he assured me that we had not been followed. With Hanover Sue safely tucked away for the night on the high ground, I radioed in the grid coordinates of our harbor site and breathed a sigh of relief. The new team had survived its first day in the bush.

Day two, I moved the team slowly. I was drilling them on proper patrolling techniques every step of the way. There were signs everywhere of heavy enemy presence. Warning signs like resting areas for platoon-size enemy units with hootches, rice caches, trail markings, unmanned bunker complexes, and the sounds of the test-firing of weapons in distant canyons kept the team alert. Late in the afternoon, we discovered a large high-speed trail with well-armed NVA streaming down it. They were moving quickly and not worrying about noise discipline. Everything I saw led me to believe that these soldiers were not just some small isolated unit roaming around the Que Sons.

Most of day three, we tried to avoid moving on or near a couple of major trails that traversed the mountain. Crossing them was like crossing a freeway at rush hour. At one point, six of us—three pairs—had moved across a high-speed trail very quickly, then it took an hour to get a big enough break in the traffic that Ayers and Adams could cross. My nerves were constantly on edge. My men were learning fast, but the responsibility for every move the team made was clearly on Ayers's and my shoulders, because any slipup could be terminal. The closer we got to the old French road, the more NVA activity we experienced. The area was swarming with enemy soldiers.

Finally, on day four, the team reached its objective. But the area around the road had been so bombed out that my map was obsolete. I positioned the team around a stand of huge trees that appeared to have been leveled by a B-52 air strike. We were about fifty meters above the road. The stream that at one time had paralleled the road now flowed across it in a half dozen places. The road wound through an awesome, very dark, heavily canopied canyon that, according to the map, stretched to the top of the mountain. The chatter of AK-47 rifles could be heard coming out of that eerie, dark canyon. Whoever was test-firing those AK-47s did not care who heard it. It was becoming ever more evident to me that the NVA owned the Que Sons.

The strong smell of fish and rice filled the air, but the road was empty except for a few stragglers. Obviously, it was chow time. Ayers looked at me and just shook his head. We were both thinking the same thing: it was a very dangerous patrol for such a green team. We were in the mouth of the lion. The sheer numbers of NVA meant that if we made any kind of contact at all, the team would take heavy casualties. We were not on terrain that was very defendable, and it was not just a battalion-size NVA unit that was on the move. The enemy was occupying the Que Sons. They were strong and organized. This was a regiment, with enemy units moving at will all over the mountains. Ayers and I were taking no chances. At last light, we had the men of Hanover Sue crawl on their hands and knees into another tangled mess of downed trees where we harbored up for the night. Nothing human would be able to sneak up on us in the dark without making a racket.

Vietnamese voices and other noises familiar in a war zone filled the canyon late into the night. I spent most of the night thinking of where, without being discovered, I would position the team tomorrow to monitor the traffic on the road. At dawn, the team recamouflaged, secured equipment, and waited to move on my command. The new guys were extremely sober and alert. It was as though they had grown up overnight. Their noise discipline was perfect. They were becoming Force Recon Marines, and that gave Ayers and me some confidence in them.

I had decided to move to a slightly higher position, one that was more defendable, about one hundred meters to the north, where another stand of trees had been knocked down. Using a narrow woodcutter trail, I took point and slowly moved the team. But as I stepped out of some waist-high undergrowth, my boot settled onto a high-speed trail. Before I could step back to check for movement, an armed NVA trail monitor walked to within ten feet of me. He had his back to me. A trail monitor's job was to direct traffic during large NVA movements. I froze. Suddenly a large enemy movement began. As I observed all the antennas and communications wire slung over the shoulders of the passing NVA, I was reminded of my recent conversation with Wayne Rollings. The next thing I saw made the hair on my neck stand up. An elite security force, walking in groups of twos and fives, began to pass in front of the trail monitor. I was still in the open, at the edge of the high-speed trail, just ten feet behind the trail monitor. Only the trail monitor shielded the elite force from looking right into my eyes. They were not expecting me to be there, so it was not registering who I actually was. I could see the barrel of Wix's M-16 rifle sticking out next to my left elbow, and I prayed Wix would maintain discipline and not open up on the column. I counted over sixty enemy pass in front of the trail monitor. I finally mustered up the courage to make a back-up motion with my left hand. Immediately, Wix's M-16 barrel moved out of my peripheral vision. Hanover Sue backed down the woodcutter trail without making a sound. My count had gone over a hundred by the time the security force had moved through. The older-looking senior officers in the group especially caught my attention. Several of them were wearing side arms and not carrying any equipment at all. I made a mental note of their uniforms, which didn't seem to bear any rank.

Before I could take my first step backward, an NVA soldier, loaded down with landline communications wire, made eye contact with me. "No," I breathed as I started to squeeze the trigger on my weapon. The enemy soldier's mouth fell open. His eyes were glued on me. Then, for no apparent reason, he just kept moving without drawing attention to my presence behind the trail monitor. I eased up on the trigger, backed onto the narrow trail, and melted into the jungle without otherwise being noticed. My heart was pounding so hard that I feared the NVA could hear it. For some reason, the NVA soldier had given me a pass. He probably couldn't believe his eyes. He probably thought, What would an American be doing on a high-speed trail, standing behind a trail monitor in the middle of an NVA regiment?

It was hard to believe, but the safest place for Hanover Sue was back in the area with all the downed trees. The bombed-out mess had become a sanctuary for us. We were right under the noses of a regiment-size NVA unit. From our position among the fallen trees above the road, Ayers and I made notes about weapons, uniforms, and numbers of enemy soldiers using the road. We radioed back information on every aspect of the enemy's presence. The numbers were incredible, and by day's end, the count had reached over four hundred. Ayers wrote a note to me when the movement finally ceased: "Happy Fourth of July, Lieutenant." Sure enough, it was the Fourth of July 1969, a day neither of us would soon forget.

Late in the afternoon, we got word that when the enemy movement stopped, a CH-46 would land on the road to extract us. The team would have to come out of hiding and run in the open for about fifty meters to board the chopper. After what we had observed on the road that day, it seemed like an impossible request. Realizing there really wasn't any other way out, I waited for the road to clear. When the road had been empty for a half hour, we got orders to make a run for it. Once the team broke into the open, two Cobra helicopters showed up, tail to tail, at treetop level above the road, firing miniguns and rockets in both directions down the road. I kept the team in front of me, yelling, "Go, go, go, move it, move it!" Then a CH-46 touched down on the road, and the team, without breaking stride, ran right up the tail ramp. The big bird did not spend more than twenty seconds on the ground before it was back in the air, flying the team home to Hill 34. It all happened so fast, I didn't think the NVA realized that the choppers had just picked up a recon team. They probably thought that the choppers had spotted some of their men using the road. To me, the dark canyon was the body of the lion. I was confident that we had sneaked into and out of the lion's mouth. Playing around the mouth of the canyon was dangerous; going into the canyon would be like allowing the lion to swallow you.

What the team had discovered would prove to be invaluable in the days ahead. As soon as I landed on Hill 34, I was handed another operation order to return into the Que Sons and try to capture a prisoner. Hanover Sue's sightings had obviously caught someone's attention either at III MAF or MACV. Two days to put together a prisoner grab was not much time, especially with an inexperienced team. I still remembered my first patrol with Rollings and the experience of being surrounded in the elephant grass with an NVA prisoner. There has to be a better way, I thought.

To my surprise, neither Major Simmons nor Captain Williams was on Hill 34 the two days I was preparing for the prisoner grab. Simmons was at III MAF in meetings. And once again, Williams was on Okinawa scrounging gear for the company. Ayers and I went about on our own to plan and carry out the mission. The two of us sat on the wooden deck attached to the officers' hootch, war-gaming the mission. Between swigs of beer, we bounced ideas off one another. We had become close friends over the months, and with the other lieutenants gone, we got even closer. Finally, after two hours of beers and ideas, we had agreed on a plan.

Ayers said, "You're right, Lieutenant, damn it. We'll go down to the lowlands at the base of the mountain. We'll pick the little bastard right off that busy road in Antenna Valley. We're gonna get a prisoner, and if any NVA screw with us, we'll blow them all away, damn it. Give me another beer."

I fumbled through a bunch of empty cans, looked at Ayers, and just started laughing. Finally I said, "Hell, Sarge, there ain't any more beer; we drank it all." We looked down at the deck. It was strewn with what appeared to be at least a case of empty beer cans.

Two days later, at first light, a CH-46 landed in a secluded clearing at the base of the Que Son Mountains on the western edge of Antenna Valley. Hanover Sue quickly exited the bird. The big chopper quickly lifted out of the zone and flew low level out of the area without appearing even to have landed. With the shadows of the Que Son mountains behind us, we moved up on the trail. We had monitored that busy route from the observation post across the valley. The ground around the trail was still scarred from all the artillery we had called in on it a month earlier. Within minutes, an NVA officer and his aide came walking down the trail. The element of surprise was completely in our favor. I smiled and chuckled, said "Gotcha" under my breath, when I gave the signal to execute the grab. Horn and Adams stepped with me on the trail and shoved their M-16s in the faces of the two NVA, taking them captive. With precision, we merely did an about-face, reversing the order of the patrol. Ayers took point, and Adams took tail-end Charlie. Horn and I took charge of the prisoners, putting them in the middle of the patrol. We marched them back to our insert LZ, and within seconds, we were boarding a CH-46 helicopter and leaving the area with our prisoners. Without having fired a shot. Bold, decisive action had made it seem easy.

By the time the team landed on the hill, two intelligence officers from III MAF were waiting to take charge of the prisoners. Ayers and I handed over the NVA officer and his aide. When I checked my watch, it was only 0730 hours. I said to Ayers, "There are no officers around, why don't you come and eat breakfast with me at the officers' mess, and we can talk." With a big important smile, Ayers replied, "Don't mind if I do, Lieutenant. I'll follow you." Ayers made a sweeping gesture toward the officers' mess hall. I turned and congratulated the team, then gave them the rest of the day off.

While Ayers and I were enjoying our second omelettes, a corporal from the company operation section showed up. He excused himself and handed me another operation order. I ignored it while I continued my conversation with Ayers. We were savoring the morning's victory. The hot coffee and a table full of hot food made for a grand banquet. When we had finished gorging ourselves and had pushed away from the table, I finally picked up the new order. I rolled it up and tapped the palm of my hand with it, saying, "We'll talk about this tonight on the deck. You bring the beer."

"Yes, sir," Ayers replied.

The scene on the deck with Ayers and me would be repeated over and over. We would sit, sipping our beer and planning patrols to take advantage of our insertion techniques. We knew we were on a roll. We also knew that it could all end with one moment's carelessness, so I continued to stress the basics. The team understood that I would not tolerate any breach of discipline in the field, and I continued to levy fines for any careless noise on patrol and dropped the money off at an orphanage in Da Nang.

Ayers always said, "Lieutenant, let's enjoy the ride while it lasts, 'cause when it's over, it's over."

Hanover Sue continued to prosper. We ran four patrols in the Que Sons in the month of July, a total of twenty days in enemy-controlled territory, five days at a time. Using helicopter inserts on the reverse side of the mountain range and moving the team quickly along narrow ridge-lines earned us the nickname "Ridge Runners." The wing was no longer prepping our zones, and insert choppers were not taking fire. We tried to pick landing zones where we knew there would be no NVA. It was hard to believe how much territory a team could cover in a day if it didn't have to go to ground because the NVA had been tipped off to our insertion by the sounds of the wing prepping the LZ. We could pop up miles away from the insert zone at will. Most of the time, the NVA did not have a clue that we were even in the area. Wix, Horn, and Adams became accomplished point men. Ayers cumshawed a CAR-15 rifle with a fifty-round magazine from a CIA special operations group, and the firepower was awesome with that weapon on point. The weeks wore on, and Hanover Sue kept producing large volumes of intelligence in the Que Sons. By the time the other lieutenants returned, Ayers and I knew the Que Sons very well.

On every patrol, I planned a day to watch the road at the mouth of that dark canyon that stretched to the top of the Que Son Mountains. I had a sense of foreboding about that canyon. Ayers and I both felt that if Hanover Sue ever ventured beyond the mouth of that dark place, we would never return. So hour after hour, we just sat and watched as NVA units walked up the road and disappeared into the forbidden canyon. During one of those vigils, a pattern began to develop. The security force, and the senior officers they protected, passed by on the road late in the morning. We watched them disappear into the dark canyon. We observed them coming out of the canyon late in the afternoon, headed in the opposite direction. Ayers and I decided to stay and monitor the road one more day. Sure enough, the guard and the senior officers passed by again, in the morning going into the canyon and in the afternoon coming out of it. We figured they must be moving between two command posts that were not very far apart. Obviously they did not want to travel in the dark, so their headquarters must have been within an hour's march in either direction. I figured that taking out the elite group was doable, but it would require a heavy-duty reinforced team with some real gunfighters on it. I knew Rollings would want a piece of the action just as soon as he returned from Okinawa. He had described the group right down to their high-and-tight haircuts, AK-47s with jungle sling, and walking in formation.

Hanover Sue could not handle all the possibilities in the Que Sons. I didn't think our missions could go on much longer, given the number of enemy sightings we were reporting to the 1st Marine Division, who had the 5th and 7th Marines working in the An Hoa Basin. Just about the time I started feeling uncomfortable about returning to the dark canyon, Ayers and I found a new fishing pond. While patrolling during the first week of August, between two low ridgelines, we found a trail that the NVA were using to walk between the Que Son Valley, Hep Duc, and Antenna Valley. The route was easy to monitor and not nearly as dangerous as the one to the dark canyon. The sightings were so rich on that route that Major Simmons needed desperately for the other lieutenants to return. He wanted to keep the area under constant surveillance by flip-flopping teams in and out of the area. That would ensure that 1st Force would maintain a constant surveillance of the NVA's movements. During the month of July, Hanover Sue had succeeded in opening up the entire Que Son Mountains with an array of vantage points from which to monitor the enemy's movement. Now, with all the lieutenants due back, Simmons planned to flood the area with Force Recon teams. He wasn't sure exactly what we had found out there, but he sensed it was big.

CHAPTER 10

The Prisoner Grab

By the first week of August, all the 1st Force lieutenants had returned to Hill 34. Randy Champe and Jim Ritchie returned from scuba school in the Philippines. They were tan, in the best shape of their lives, and ready for action. Ric Miller was back from his thirty-day leave in California and preoccupied with a girl he had met. With his four tours in Vietnam, the other lieutenants figured Miller had earned the right to have a woman in his life. Rollings and Lowder returned from jump school on Okinawa. The joke was that the sun didn't shine in the Sucran officers club, and that was why they didn't have tans.

Bob Hansen, the communications officer, returned from setting up radio relays to service the patrols in the Que Sons. During an attack on one of the relays, a piece of shrapnel from an NVA rocket had nearly killed him. He had a wife and son at home, so after some prompting from Major Simmons, he decided against another tour. We lieutenants wished him well in a party at our new officers club, The Leaky Teaky. Someone asked Hansen that night how the hell the space program could talk to someone on the moon by radio. Everyone knew Bob had struggled to keep the old PRC-25 radios we used from falling apart. And, despite all his efforts, at best they could only reach a few miles. So we spent the whole night dogging the moon landing and their great communications system.

I looked pretty tired and worn out compared to the other lieutenants who had returned after over a month's absence from the intensity of the battle. What I had going was the edge that comes when there are no distractions to take your mind off patrolling. My senses were at their peak from spending weeks in the bush. I knew I was at the highest point of my game. I also knew that I couldn't remain there forever. Nobody could.

When I tried to share what we had uncovered in the Que Sons, the lieutenants sat listening with what bordered on disbelief. Then Rollings weighed in with his sighting of the elite unit. Without Rollings's support, I would have had a difficult time convincing the lieutenants how active things had gotten in their absence. Not that it had not been active before, but if we flooded the Que Sons with Force Recon teams, there was bound to be an appropriate enemy response. There were rumors that the NVA 44 Headquarters Group, another name for the legendary Front Four, was definitely around the Que Sons. The intelligence officers at III MAF confirmed the presence of some form of high-ranking NVA, apparently formulating a plan for a late-summer offensive. The NVA officer that Hanover Sue had captured a few weeks earlier had confirmed the presence of high-ranking NVA officers in the Que Sons.

The more Rollings and I compared notes on that elite security unit, the more committed we got to going after them. MACV and III MAF had a lot of names for the NVA brass calling the shots in the I Corps area. I didn't really care what they called them. I just knew that I had seen those guys, with their briefcases and beautiful women, going in and out of the dark canyon. On one occasion, I could almost have reached out and touched them. I believed they were worth killing, and so did Rollings, and that's all we needed to take a shot at it.

I knew where I wanted to run my next patrol and what I wanted to accomplish. And I knew it would take twice the usual number of qualified men to successfully accomplish the mission, a prisoner grab. I had found a place across the river from the Que Sons on a short two-day patrol I had run a couple of weeks earlier. All the traffic on the trail was obviously leading into the Que Sons. There was an old woodcutter's trail that led across the top of a narrow ridgeline. I planned to land on the reverse side of the mountain with a twelve-man team. Then we would walk to the top of the mountain, pick up the woodcutter's trail, and move quickly along the ridge. I would drop four of my men at the intersection of the trail and a spur that led to a disused high-speed trail. I planned to lead the eight-man prisoner-grab element down the spur to a well-traveled high-speed trail. I had traveled the route before and noted that it had great possibilities for such a mission. Once we had the prisoner, we would move back up the mountain and link up with our rear security. Then we would retrace our route across the narrow ridgeline, dropping over the reverse side of the mountain. We could then be extracted with our prisoner from the same spot that we were inserted into. This plan was more complex than just stepping out on the trail at the base of the Que Sons and grabbing a couple of NVA. We noticed over the week that we rarely saw any groups smaller than a half-dozen NVA walking the trails. To get another prisoner, we needed a place that we could hide, watch, and escape from. I felt that this was that place.

I studied the faces of the other lieutenants as I shared the plan. I understood that the actual grab might get real physical. It would have to be quick and decisive. Miller's head was still in San Francisco. Ritchie had not yet completely recovered from the chopper crash. Rollings was not interested in a prisoner grab; he wanted a piece of the elite NVA group and was headed back to the dark canyon. Champe needed to pick up the pieces of his team after the loss of Private First Class Murphy and the wounding of Sergeant Ott. That left Lowder, who seemed more than willing to add his best men to the mission and give it a try. So, while the other lieutenants slept, Lowder and I put together every detail of the plan.

Lowder and I reported to Major Simmons's office early the next morning. Simmons sat quietly sipping his coffee while I began to describe the patrol. Lowder provided the color commentary, how the prisoner would be escorted off the trail and up the mountain. The more we shared the details of the patrol, the more encouraged we became. We planned to place two-man flank security with small radios on either side of the acquisition element of the patrol. Lowder and I assigned ourselves the role of actually stepping out on the trail and grabbing the prisoner. Using coded radio signals from our flank security, we felt it would be possible to choose when we could grab the enemy soldier. We wanted an obvious NVA officer, so less important enemy soldiers would be allowed to pass through the ambush. I spoke cautiously when I suggested, "Sir, if the flank security was armed with silenced M-16 rifles, we could quell any interruptions without blowing the mission." Simmons only nodded as he listened carefully. We knew that III MAF needed more firsthand information about the summer offensive and Front Four's presence in the area, and it was fairly easy to count NVA noses; I felt that it was time to grab one of the NVA and find out what was really going on.

Simmons did not hesitate to give the prisoner grab a green light. Nothing that we requested for the patrol was denied, not even the silenced weapons and special hand-held radios. We were also guaranteed an immediate extract if the patrol got into deep trouble. We were given a week to plan and rehearse the mission.

Lowder, at six feet five, had played football for Northern Illinois University, and I had played linebacker in the Far Western Conference for San Francisco State, so we knew we had the natural abilities and instincts for the mission. Our strengths complemented one another.

Over the next few days, we spent many hours brainstorming every possible scenario. Night after night, and often into the early-morning hours, we discussed the mechanics of the mission until we were actually completing one another's sentences.

We trained the team to move on particular commands, just like the snap of a football. Flank security would signal Lowder that the playing field was safe by giving one beep on the handheld radio. Lowder would check with both flanks before stepping on the trail to cover me as I executed the grab. I would emphasize that "nobody moves until I shout, 'Go!' Then both right- and left-flank securities seal the trail. If a superior force tries to overrun us, you are to blow your claymore mines to stop them. Do you understand?"

The men answered in unison, "Yes, sir."

Then Lowder asked, "What is the first thing that flank security does when it reaches its position five meters to the left and right of the acquisition team?"

Flank security answered, "Set the claymores and then establish radio contact with Lieutenant Lowder, sir."

I continued the quiz, asking, "Do we want just any NVA soldier?"

Flank security answered, "No, sir, we want an NVA officer."

Lowder shouted, "Who is my right-flank security?"

Private Adams and Private Horn responded, "We are, sir."

Lowder shouted a second time, "Who is my left-flank security?"

Private Harrington and Lance Corporal Marr responded, "We are, sir."

Then I took over, asking, "Where do my radioman and corpsman set up?"

Doc Andrews answered, while Lance Corporal Foley nodded, "Two meters behind you and Lieutenant Lowder, sir." Ayers did not allow the question concerning the rear security to be asked. The salty sergeant merely piped in, "Sir, this sergeant will take these three men and assume your rear security at the top of the ridgeline at the intersection of the two trails. We will harbor up on the ridgeline and not allow the enemy access to your escape route."

The hours of preparation turned into days, and the days turned into a week. Finally, on August 9, Hanover Sue was ready to execute the mission. The team, armed with four silenced M-16 rifles in the hands of the flank security, and a silenced Smith & Wesson holstered on my hip, boarded the CH-46. We flew over the Que Sons, crossed the river, and landed on the reverse side of a mountain. There was an air of confidence in the team. They were prepared for whatever they might encounter.

The insert of the team on the reverse side of the mountain late in the afternoon was routine and went well. The move along the narrow ridgeline went swiftly as the team moved without any danger of being ambushed because of the cliffs that fell off both sides of the mountain. I motioned Ayers to drop out of the column at the intersection of the two trails and assume rear security for the team with his assigned men. At last light, Hanover Sue moved into a harbor site near the intersection of the old and new high-speed trails, where the mission would be executed. The quiet of the warm evening was interrupted intermittently by loud voices and AK-47 fire echoing out of the mountains. The activity served as a reminder to Lowder and me that we had entered into a very dangerous North Vietnamese stronghold. The NVA were bold and confident, which meant they had the manpower and firepower to handle most situations.

We heard voices on the trail throughout the night. Obviously, the NVA were moving large units into the Que Sons under the cover of darkness. An hour before dawn, Lowder and I were wide awake on the jungle floor, trying to recall any detail we might have forgotten. We sat up at first light and listened intently for enemy movement on the trail. The adrenaline began to pump as we quietly slipped into our equipment. There would be no breakfast that morning. I signaled my teammates to apply fresh camouflage paint to their faces. A few minutes after dawn, the men of Hanover Sue stood to their feet. We were ready to move into position along the busy high-speed trail.

I cautiously assumed point, slowly moving the team the last twenty meters down to the objective. Horn and Adams waited for the signal to break off to the right and take up flank security. I moved one step to the right side of the trail without taking my eyes off the jungle in front of me. I motioned Lowder to take point. Barely breathing, Lowder stepped forward as his eyes searched every inch of the terrain between him and the objective. Movement had ceased on the trail and now a little bit of luck was all Hanover Sue needed to slip into position before the traffic resumed. I motioned right and then left with one hand while my other hand held a firm grip on the Swedish-K 9mm machine gun. Harrington and Marr moved to the left while Horn and Adams moved to the right. In near perfect silence, both flank-security teams set their claymore mines facing outboard and covering the trail, then moved out of the backblast area directly behind the mines and assumed positions a few feet off the trail in the lush jungle foliage. After giving the flanks precisely ninety seconds to set up, Lowder and I eased to within three feet of the trail, using the thick foliage at the intersection to cover our position. Andrews and Foley positioned themselves a few feet deeper into the jungle, directly behind Lowder and me.

Within seconds of moving into position, I heard movement to my right, and in my mind I cursed, thinking Horn and Adams were getting restless. Lowder, lying on his side, had his ear glued to his handheld radio as he tried to make contact with the flank security. Lowder, slightly behind me, began moving when the first group of enemy soldiers walked by from the right. Fearing that Lowder's movement might cause the squad of heavily armed NVA to spot us, I held my breath. I had already loosened the Ranger straps off my shoulders and unbuckled my cartridge belt so that I could move quickly for the grab. My rifle hung from my neck on a jungle strap, allowing both of my hands to be free if I had to physically subdue the prisoner. With one of my free hands, I carefully reached behind me and squeezed Lowder's leg. Lowder froze as a second group of NVA passed in front of me. I was close enough to reach through the bushes and touch the enemy troops. I could hear their heavy breathing, smell their sweat, and see every detail of their uniforms and equipment.

Finally the last of the squad of NVA moved through the ambush site. Lowder, unable to communicate with his right-flank security, shook his head in disgust. Signals from Harrington and Marr, on the left, were coming through perfectly. Lowder mouthed the words without speaking out loud, "Come on, Horn, talk to me." Without the radio signal, we were blind on our right flank. We had no idea what was approaching from that direction. Lowder and I did not know whether it was safe to reach out and grab a prisoner or not. We had little time to assess the situation. Suddenly from the left flank the sound of music could be heard coming down the trail. Harrington's signal was one beep, which meant let them pass. Lowder squeezed my arm once. I had unholstered my silenced pistol and had it aimed at the trail with the barrel pointed left. Through the sight on the pistol I watched as a man and woman came into the frame. The man carried a portable radio that was blasting rock and roll music. As he approached our position, he stopped directly in front of me and coughed. The man's face was eighteen inches from my silenced pistol. I took up the slack on the trigger and began to squeeze as my eyes and the man's eyes met. Suddenly an American voice bellowed through the radio, "This is your South Vietnam special services station," and then a woman's voice, "Good morning, Vietnam, this is Chris Noel." Chris Noel was the dream girl of every guy in Vietnam. When other celebrities had betrayed those who chose to serve in Vietnam, Chris Noel had back-burnered her career in Hollywood to entertain GIs from one end of Vietnam to the other. I eased off the trigger. Which would prove to be a good decision as things developed. Chris's voice had kept me from blowing our plan. The woman gently touched the man and said something in Vietnamese. The man responded, and they moved on down the trail as though they had not seen anything.

Perspiration flowed down my camouflaged face,

soaking the collar of my jungle utilities. I was not sure if the man had made eye contact with me or not. I took my eyes off the trail for a beat and turned my head toward Lowder. I mouthed the words "I think he saw me," pointing to my own eyes and then making a slicing motion across my neck with my index finger. Before Lowder could respond, the sound of someone walking toward us from our blind side to the right froze both of us. I slowly turned my head so that my eyes could line up with the trail. Off in the distance, the music from the man's radio could be faintly heard, so I knew it could not be him again. Thoughts rushed through my mind: Maybe he saw me; I should have shot him or taken him prisoner; maybe he reported our presence to some NVA troops moving down the trail.

Before Lowder and I could exchange glances, three enemy soldiers were on the trail right in front of us. I allowed my right hand to take a firm grip on the Swedish-K. Through the jungle undergrowth, we observed the three figures on the trail. One NVA lay on a pole stretcher. He was in full uniform. His olive-drab utilities bore no rank. His pith helmet, resting on his shoulders, dangled from a thin leather cord tied around his neck. I searched every inch of the soldier's uniform for some sign of his rank. The mission specifically commanded the team to capture an officer, and nothing less than that was satisfactory. When the NVA rolled over on the stretcher, there, on his hip, attached to his cartridge belt, was the clue to his rank: a holstered pistol. Only NVA officers wore pistols in the field. The two men accompanying the NVA officer were stretcher bearers assigned to carry the ailing man. I looked at Lowder out of the corner of my eye and grinned. Lowder nodded, gave a thumbs-up sign, and followed me onto the trail.

Like lightning, we burst onto the trail. I yelled, "Go," and both left- and right-flank security sealed the trail. Lowder yelled, *"Dung lai,"* which in Vietnamese means stop. The confused stretcher bearers dropped their pole and ran, leaving the NVA officer stranded in the middle of the trail. Until we had stepped onto the trail, we could not see what was on our right flank. It was no longer a mystery. There, between the lieutenants, Horn, and Adams, stood a column of heavily armed NVA. The element of surprise that was on our side quickly vanished as the enemy soldiers began to raise their weapons. The soldier on the stretcher immediately scrambled to his feet and ran down the trail, but his escape was blocked by Harrington and Marr. I saw an enemy rifle trained on me and knew I could not turn fast enough to protect myself, but Lowder opened fire, cutting down the man and five other NVA as he emptied a full magazine through his M-16 rifle. Horn and Adams killed two more enemy soldiers with two silenced bursts of fire. Seeing another platoon-size element advancing up the trail, Horn pulled Adams back into the jungle with him and reached for the clacker of the claymore mine. The explosion sent a deadly spray of ball bearings into the ranks of the NVA.

Just as the claymore exploded, I made a game-saving tackle on the NVA officer, who had tried to run past me to escape. I struggled on the ground with the NVA prisoner, who was reaching for his cartridge belt. The holster looked empty, but I feared he might be going for a grenade. Trying to subdue the prisoner with one hand while maintaining a grip on my Swedish-K with the other, I inadvertently squeezed the trigger, shooting a perfectly straight line on the ground between myself and the struggling prisoner. I finally ran out of patience and unloaded my forearm hard against the NVA's jaw. The enemy soldier went limp. Right on schedule, Doc Andrews moved onto the trail and pulled me to my feet. Then both of us pulled the dazed enemy officer off the ground and tied his hands behind him. Andrews removed the prisoner's cartridge belt and handed me a number of documents from a canvas purse tied around his waist. I stuffed them into a pocket on my jungle utility trousers and buttoned it shut. The prisoner went ballistic when he became separated from the papers. He fell back to the ground, screaming and resisting Andrews.

The backblast of the claymore had thrown smoke and dust up and down the trail, and Lowder strained to see through the gray haze that hung over us. He was about to open up again on two shadowy figures, but at the last second, he identified them: Horn and Adams. "Let's move it! Harrington, help Andrews with the prisoner," I said.

Harrington, a black, six-foot-six Marine from the mean streets of Detroit, moved to Andrews's side, reached down and grabbed the NVA officer by the throat, jerked him to his feet, and growled, "Walk, asshole."

Hanover Sue's plan was working almost perfectly. Although we had been badly outnumbered, the team's rehearsal and good reactions under pressure had netted us a prisoner. Sergeant Ayers was in communication with the radioman, Foley, as the team assembled and started back up the mountain. But still the prisoner refused to cooperate, throwing himself to the ground and screaming in Vietnamese, so Doc Andrews decided to tape his mouth shut. Unfortunately, the prisoner bit into the corpsman's thumb and refused to let go. We decided to carry the unwilling prisoner to the top of the mountain; his resistance was using up valuable time.

Hanover Sue had plucked its prisoner out of a company-size movement. The NVA now had a chance to regroup and were busy dispatching squads to track us down before we escaped with one of their own. The chase was on! But the prisoner's struggles brought the recon team to a complete halt as NVA squads began to fan out in every direction in pursuit. The prisoner's voice echoed off the mountain, providing the squads with the location of our position.

Anticipating that the NVA might be able to move ahead of Hanover Sue and cut us off from rear security, Ayers had moved down the mountain. His instincts were right; he spotted a half-dozen NVA taking up positions between his rear security element and the rest of us. He quickly alerted Foley, who relayed the message to me. We were effectively cut off from our escape route. I signaled the team to form a perimeter while Lowder grabbed the radio handset from Foley and called for air support. There was no response to Lowder's first plea.

A second time Lowder radioed, "Recon team in trouble, need air support. Over."

This time a voice came over the radio: "Recon team, this is Hostage Jim. Can you give me your call sign and position? Over?"

"Hostage Jim this is Hanover Sue. It's sure good to hear your voice, buddy. I'm at grid 861480. Do you copy? Over."

Hostage Jim calmly radioed back, "Hanover Sue, I copy. What can I do for you?"

With a big grin on his face, Lowder replied, "Hostage Jim, we've got bad guys all around us down here. We have one NVA prisoner. Over!"

"No wonder you're surrounded," Hostage Jim said. "Sounds like you kidnapped one of Hanoi's finest. I'm over your position now. I see people moving on a trail down there. Is that you, Hanover Sue?"

"That's a negative, Hostage Jim," Lowder responded excitedly. "Those are bad guys on the trail."

Chuckling, Hostage Jim said, "Well, let's get them off the trail permanently." With that transmission Hostage Jim brought his spotter plane, an OV-10 Bronco, in at almost treetop level and raked the trail with machine-gun fire and rockets, mowing down a dozen enemy troops.

Suddenly Ayers's voice came up on the radio. "Hostage Jim, be advised you have friendlies on top of the ridgeline. I have marked my position with an air panel. Do you copy?"

Hostage Jim responded immediately. "I copy that. Friendlies on the ridgeline. I see your air panel."

Ayers continued, "Hostage Jim, we have NVA forty meters from the air panel on a compass heading of 164 degrees. Over." Hostage Jim could be heard circling above the canopy, but there was no response to Ayers's last transmission.

Several minutes went by and suddenly Major Simmons's voice came over the radio. "Hanover Sue, this is King Fish Six. Do you copy?"

Lowder replied, "Ah, roger, King Fish, I've got you loud and clear."

Simmons got right to the point. "Hanover Sue, prepare for a SPIE rig extract. We will take the acquisition element of the team out first, over." Lowder confirmed the order and passed the word to get ready for the SPIE rig.

While we prepared our nylon ropes and snap links for the extract, Phantom jets and Cobra gunships began to deliver accurate firepower on the enemy. The Phantoms concentrated their bombing runs on the trail below the team while the Cobra gunships fired rockets at the NVA squad that had moved between Ayers and the acquisition team. The scream of the jet engines on the Phantoms was deafening. The concussion from the five-hundred-pound bombs hitting the trail lifted the Marines off the ground. The smell of gunpowder and explosives filled the air. One of Ayers's men took a piece of shrapnel through the wrist from one of the Cobra's rockets. The angry sergeant hollered over the radio, "Keep that crap off us, damn it! You just wounded one of my men."

Hostage Jim came back up on the net, apologizing to Ayers for the close call.

Just as the Phantoms and Cobras pulled away from the mountain, the sound of a single CH-46 helicopter could be heard just above the treetops, directly over Hanover Sue. Doc Andrews had tied a nylon rope around the chest area of the prisoner with a snap link attached to it. The SPIE rig strap was dropped through a hole in the canopy. Lowder and I waited until we saw that the entire team and the prisoner were firmly attached to the rig before snapping ourselves on. With the Phantoms and Cobras off station, the NVA began to fire on the extract helicopter. Rather than pulling us straight up through the hole in the canopy the chopper pilot moved the big bird forward to gain extra power for the lift. This maneuver threw Hanover Sue into a gully full of dead trees and boulders, wrapping me around the trunk of a downed tree and driving the Swedish-K into my rib cage. I felt the bones in my legs about ready to break as I violently ricocheted off trees and rocks. I can only describe this experience and my injuries as if I had been in a very bad motorcycle accident. The pilot finally gained control of the 46 and pulled the team straight up, but we were snapping branches off the trees as we broke through the canopy. Horn's and Adams's silenced weapons were torn from their hands, Horn's striking me in the head and knocking me unconscious. Damn, and I was having such a good day.

When I regained consciousness, the team was about fifteen hundred feet above the jungle floor. I surveyed the situation through glassy eyes. I counted and recounted my men and was amazed to find that they had all stayed attached to the rig. Lowder was hanging next to me. He, too, had been counting the men. "They're all on, buddy! We did it. We got that sucker out of there," Lowder yelled.

I kept checking the prisoner for some sign of life. When he didn't open his eyes or change expressions, I started to become concerned. Doc Andrews was hanging off the rig next to the NVA. I yelled, "Hey, Doc, is he alive?"

Andrews looked up at me with a big grin and yelled back, "Yes, sir, he's just sleeping from the three shots of morphine I gave him after the bastard bit me." Relief came over me. Once Ayers and his men got plucked off the ridgeline and were home with the rest of the team, it would be time to celebrate.

The CH-46 helicopter pilot was commanded to land the team at An Hoa by some colonel at III MAF's intelligence G-2 section. The team was gently set down on the metal runway. The colonel greeted Lowder and me as we unsnapped ourselves from the SPIE rig. We saluted the colonel, who proceeded to identify himself. When the suggestion was made that the team surrender the prisoner to the MAF's interrogator at An Hoa, Lowder and I refused; our orders were to return to Hill 34 with the prisoner. Simmons had spelled that out very clearly in our operation order, and we did not want to deviate from fully completing our mission. The colonel, showing full respect for what we had accomplished, decided to merely fly the team and the prisoner to Hill 34 in his chopper. We agreed.

Hanover Sue guarded the prisoner and nervously waited for a report on how Sergeant Ayers and the other men were doing. The team broke out in a wild celebration as Ayers and his men appeared on the horizon, dangling beneath another CH-46. The safe return of the team was another miracle for Hanover Sue.

Hanover Sue's twelve-man team, one NVA officer in our possession, boarded the III MAF chopper upon the colonel's invitation and was flown to Hill 34 in style. Major Simmons looked like a coach who had just won the big game. He saluted the colonel but kind of looked through him. He wanted to shake his lieutenants' hands and congratulate the rest of the team. Simmons did not care about the politics involved with any senior officer. He was aloof from it.

When Lowder and I walked down the ramp of the chopper with the prisoner, Simmons was the first one to greet us. He wanted to know why I was bleeding and bruised. When he heard that the team had been dragged through the trees he got angry. "Who in the hell was flying that chopper?" he asked. I tried to explain the accident away, but Simmons would not hear of it. He was determined to get to the bottom of the screwup. He went straight to the pilots and said, "We can't have our men dragged through the trees when we use the SPIE rig. The pilots who do these extracts must be experienced in using the rig. They have got to train with it and learn how to use it so as not to risk my men's lives in the field."

The III MAF colonel nodded in agreement and said, "Major, I have my counterintelligence team with me. We need to see what the prisoner knows. I would like my men to interrogate him right now." Simmons was still upset about the way the SPIE rig extract was handled, but he quickly composed himself and ordered us to turn over to the intelligence team the prisoner and the papers he'd been carrying.

Although the prisoner was still heavily sedated from the morphine, he began to supply some key intelligence information. While on a stretcher next to the helo pad, the NVA officer admitted to the counterintelligence team that he was a major in the 2d NVA Division. He further admitted he was a courier and had been carrying important documents, the nature of which he refused to discuss. One of the intelligence officers, a vicious-looking Korean Marine, kept having to smack the prisoner on his arm and talk tough to keep him awake. In Vietnamese, a second intelligence officer asked, "What is the 2d NVA Division trying to do? What are they doing in the Que Sons?" The prisoner slurred his words, and the intelligence officer smacked him again to keep him awake. He then repeated his question. This time, the prisoner gave him an answer. The prisoner said very clearly in Vietnamese, "We have come to fight."

The Korean interrogator started to really rough him up, saying, "Fight where? Fight when?"

The colonel said, "That's enough for now." Then he handed the Vietnamese-speaking intelligence officer the papers I had captured. "I want to know the nature of these documents just as quickly as possible," he said.

Right around the time that we pulled off the prisoner grab, something in the realm of international politics took place in Vietnam that would put even more pressure on 1st Force: President Richard Milhous Nixon arrived in Vietnam unannounced. The president's visit would have a profound effect on 1st Force's mission in the I Corps area of Vietnam.

Nixon's visit would cause a trickle-down effect, from General Abrams at MACV in Saigon, to General Nickerson at III MAF, to Maj. Roger Simmons on Hill 34, to 1st Force Recon Company in the field. The president stated emphatically in his meeting with Abrams, "America's allies, Asian nations included, will have to bear the burden of their own defenses against conventional attack." Then he added, "General Abrams, I plan to tell the American people when I return to the capital that we will be accelerating our troop withdrawals from Vietnam." General Abrams had for months been continually pressed by Secretary of Defense Laird to accelerate Vietnamization and withdrawal. Abrams had resisted Laird on the grounds that it was dangerous to shift the burden of fighting the war too quickly to the South Vietnamese Army. Now he was being compelled to comply with the Nixon-Kissinger plan by the commander in chief himself.

General Abrams passed the word to General Nickerson at III MAF. It was obvious to everyone at III MAF that their job had become to keep the lid on the war in the I Corps area so that American troops could safely be withdrawn. First Force was doing all it could do to keep III MAF informed about the buildups of NVA troops around Da Nang and points west. Rumors were circulating that MACV, after hearing about 1st Force's string of successes, also wanted to use them on some special missions. Three MAF's Surveillance Reconnaissance Center believed that Nixon's public announcement would probably cause the NVA to become more aggressive at the tactical level of their war against South Vietnam. General Nickerson moved quickly to activate 1st Force's sister company, 3d Force. His plan was to turn 3d Force loose on the NVA from the A Shau Valley north to the Demilitarized Zone between North and South Vietnam. Neither General Abrams nor General Nickerson had much control over the timetable of the Nixon-Kissinger Vietnamization program. They would be told by the Pentagon which of their units would be withdrawn and when that withdrawal would take place.

In the midst of those major changes in American troop strength in Vietnam, the NVA began to use counterreconnaissance teams to hunt down and kill the Marine recon teams. The NVA counterreconnaissance teams dressed like recon Marines, moved in small teams, and mirrored the patrolling techniques used by the Americans. But the NVA also brought dogs and indigenous tribesmen to track the recon teams. New Russian-made radio surveillance and tracking equipment was also released against 1st Force.

First Force Recon had become the tip of the spear that was pointed right at the eye of the NVA. We were about to totally expose the NVA's plan for a summer offensive against Quang Nam Province, more specifically, Da Nang. We had pretty much pinpointed the location of Front Four, a.k.a. the 44 Headquarters Group. We just needed a little more hard evidence about the 2d NVA Division's existence and intentions in the Que Son Mountains.

As 1st Force's class of 1969, we were about to establish our legacy for time spent and battles fought during our tour in Vietnam. The magnitude of that legacy was not really under our control. We were the trigger-pullers in the jungles and mountains where the enemy moved at will. We knew firsthand the tremendous numbers of NVA in close proximity to Da Nang. Often, we felt like a voice crying in the wilderness with nobody listening. The only thing we in 1st Force had to confirm what we saw in the field was each other. It wasn't always easy to convince a weenie intelligence officer someplace "in the rear with the gear" how dangerous the situation around Da Nang really was. We continued to do our job in spite of all the political and military handicaps.

CHAPTER 11

Into the Mouth of the Lion

The morning after our prisoner grab, Lowder and I sat quietly in the hootch, cleaning weapons and sorting gear. I was trying to remove the twisted 36-round magazine from my Swedish-K 9mm assault weapon. The contusions and lacerations on my thighs and lower legs were visible beneath my tiger-stripe shorts. I was stripped to the waist, and a deep purple bruise covered my rib cage on the left side where the cold steel of my own weapon had slammed into my side upon impact with the trees. My arms, neck, and face were covered with cuts from the vines and branches that the helicopter had dragged the team through, but I was alive.

Lowder was saying, "You know, Paco, when those stretcher bearers set that guy down in front of us, you know what I was thinking?"

"I give. What?"

Without looking up, Lowder continued. "I was thinking about it being Sunday, and I knew everybody would be enjoying steak and beer for dinner back here. Then I thought if we could capture that dude right then, that we would make it back here for the beer and steak."

I clutched my bruised ribs and began to laugh as I replied, "You were thinking about steak and beer while I was thinking that guy and woman with the radio had me. You have got to be shittin' me, bro."

Just then, the door to the officers' hootch swung open and Wayne Rollings burst in, grabbed his patrolling gear off his rack, and slipped into his Ranger straps. His grease-painted face was sweaty. Clearly, he was going to the bush to do business. He picked up his M-16, cleared the chamber, gave it one last inspection. "Paco," he said, "you figure those downed trees will get me close enough to that road the NVA brass is using?"

I looked intently at him and replied, "Yeah, that'll get you close enough. That's the mouth of the lion, Wayne. Don't even think about going up that road into the dark canyon, bro, because you won't come out. That canyon is the lion's belly. Get into those trees, and you will see all you need to see." Rollings hesitated and then just nodded and headed toward the door.

Lowder yelled, "Rollings!" Wayne turned, walked back, and stood in the door of the hootch. Lowder said, "Watch your ass out there, bro." With a look of resolve, Rollings nodded, then turned around and headed out into the compound.

The sounds of the two CH-46 helicopters touching down on Hill 34's metal runway were deafening. Dust blew across the hill as the tin-roofed hootches vibrated to the beat of the rotor blades. Lunch Meat double-timed onto the chopper just as it had done dozens of times before. Rollings took a seat at one of the rear oval windows and studied his map. The chopper lifted off and headed west. Rollings's cue to move up to the cockpit came when he recognized the big horseshoe in the Thu Bon River. The horseshoe was unmistakable from the air. It meant the next discernible landmark would be the Que Son Mountains. Rollings moved forward toward the pilots to verify his landing zone on the reverse side of the mountains. He did not recognize the pilots. Rarely any longer did the lieutenants run into their old pilot buddies from the air wing; some had died in crashes, some had rotated back to the States. Nothing is ever permanent in war.

Pointing through the glass in the cockpit, Rollings said, "There it is." The bombed-out area was not the cleanest place to land, but it was hidden from the high ridgeline to the west and the valley floor to the east. Rollings liked it, and led his team quickly off the back of the 46 and under the nearby jungle canopy.

Earlier that morning, another CH-46 had deposited two Force Recon teams on the south end of the Que Sons. The teams headed in opposite directions from each other when they left the chopper. Report Card, led by Randy Champe, worked its way up to a defendable piece of high ground overlooking the high-speed trail that ran along the edge of Antenna Valley. That was the trail that Ayers and I had found earlier in the summer, the trail to which I had delivered payback for the lives of Nelson, Laken, and Vivillaqua. It was the trail that Horn, Adams, and I had stepped onto early one morning to capture an NVA officer and his aide. The trail that had drawn Simmons's attention toward the Que Sons in the first place.

Jim Ritchie took the other team, Pearl Chest, and positioned himself on high ground with an even better view of the trail. He surveilled the enemy route perfectly where it came out from beneath the jungle canopy. Nothing could move on that trail without Champe or Ritchie seeing it from two different angles. They were monitoring the key entry and exit point into and out of the Que Sons.

After just one day, the sightings of NVA by the two teams were incredible. More than five hundred well-equipped NVA troops had been spotted. Simmons felt he needed something really ironclad to prove the accuracy of what his men in the field were reporting. He settled on a set of seismic intrusion devices that could be planted next to the trail. The battery-driven gear counted the footfalls of the enemy soldiers as they walked by.

Late one afternoon, while Champe's and Ritchie's teams were still monitoring the large enemy movements, the major summoned Lowder and me to his office. He began the conversation by saying, "I thought you would like to know that your prisoner slept the last three days. We have had the intelligence spooks calling us and wanting to know what you gave that guy. It *was* just morphine, wasn't it?" We nodded. Simmons smiled and added, "Well, he finally woke up a couple of hours ago and started spilling his guts. It seems that he is a high-ranking officer from Hanoi and very well educated. He confirmed that the 90th NVA Regiment and the 44 Headquarters Group is in the area to launch a summer offensive. According to him, the Force Recon teams have been messing up their element of surprise and their ability to mass a significant number of troops in the Que Sons. They have decided to bring in dogs, counter-reconnaissance teams, and radio-signal-detection devices to hunt us down and kill us."

Simmons walked past us toward the door of his office, and over his shoulder he said, "Follow me, I've got something I want to show you." Lowder and I walked with the major to the rear of the command bunker. There on the ground, laid out carefully, on two green, military-issue, wool blankets, was the battery-operated surveillance equipment. We started laughing when we saw that they had been "camouflaged" as plastic green plants that did not resemble anything we had ever seen in the jungle. The immense posthole digger also brought a chuckle; Lowder knew only his six-foot-five-inch frame would be able to carry the tool—and then only if it was strapped to his back.

I finally turned to the major and asked, "Sir, what do you want us to do?"

The major had a big grin on his face. "Well, men, I want you to slip down to that trail Ritchie and Champe are watching and bury these devices on the edge of it. Now, I know it's a pretty busy place, but I figured you two will come up with a plan and get the job done."

Reaching down, I picked up the posthole digger by the handles and said, "Sir, could we leave this here? I think we can get them into that soft ground without any problem."

Choking back laughter, Simmons said, "Lieutenant Peters, Lieutenant Lowder, if that is your only request, then leave that piece of junk here."

Champe and Ritchie exchanged comments over their radios as they heard our chopper land at first light the next morning. Ayers liked the idea that there were three recon teams in such close proximity. He was running point on the mission because I wanted someone I knew could think quickly on his feet. Sure enough, as Ayers approached the trail several NVA passed in front of him no more than five meters away. Ayers, who was not taking any chances, opened up on them. The mortar rounds in the NVA's packs clanked as they ran down the trail. With my ear up to the radio receiver, I heard Ritchie whisper, "That's funny, your point guy opened up on them, and all they did was take a few quick steps down the trail and return to their walking pace."

"You're kidding. What do you make of that?" I asked.

"I don't know. They just ran a few steps and slowed right down and just started walking again." Perplexed, Ritchie continued, "I don't get it. Why didn't they return fire or something? This doesn't make sense." Ritchie continued, "Here comes more traffic. They should be right in front of you on the trail in about thirty seconds." Sure enough, a long column of about forty heavily armed NVA passed by, not even looking in the direction of the team.

"Are these guys crazy? Why are they ignoring us, or didn't it register with any of them who had fired at the earlier group?" I asked.

We would never be able to explain why the NVA had not picked up on our presence. Sometimes war seems just a game in which unexplainable things merely happen. The enemy troops whom Ayers had fired on probably were not communicating with the next unit that came down the trail, so 1st Force had a free ticket to bury the surveillance gear and make a clean getaway. Lowder and I decided to move the team away from the trail, loop south, and intersect the trail again about two hundred meters from our present position. I whispered to Lowder, "Let's get an aerial observer to make passes over the trail and see if we can get these guys to stop using it while we bury this crap." Lowder grabbed the radio and put out the request for air support. Within two hours, an aerial observer was flying his OV 10 Bronco up and down the trail. The NVA stopped their movements, and for the first time, the portion of the trail that was visible from the air had no enemy movement on it. Ayers and I armed then buried the devices while the rest of the team provided security. Ayers used his K-bar knife to dig a hole in the soft ground just off the edge of the trail. I dropped an electronic gadget the size of a shoe box into the hole. In a low whisper, Ayers said, "Why don't we pull a little prisoner grab while we're here, just to make it interesting."

"Don't put any ideas like that in my head. I'm still so beat up I couldn't wrestle a woman to the ground." In five minutes, the holes were being covered up, and the fake foliage was in place over their antennas to disguise them. I gave the flank security the signal to retreat, and the team melted back into the jungle. The aerial observer gained altitude and flew out of the area.

Within minutes, the NVA were back walking on the trail. The permanent observation point across Antenna Valley to the west picked up the signal from the NVA's footsteps and reported that it was loud and clear. Champe and Richie could monitor the NVA at ground level while the observation post across the valley could count them with the use of the surveillance gear, day and night.

Major Simmons now had his ironclad case. He could prove that huge numbers of NVA were moving about in the Que Son Mountains and adjacent valleys. Just as quickly as 1st Force had invaded the Que Sons with four highly qualified and experienced teams, they silently withdrew them. Rollings grudgingly withdrew after three days of monitoring the road leading into the dark canyon. The elite security unit and high-ranking command group had continued to use the road. Rollings had carefully noted the times of day that the group used the road going into and exiting the canyon.

The chopper carrying me and Lowder reached Hill 34 a couple of hours before the rest of the teams. The beer was flowing freely by the time Rollings returned late that afternoon. We laughed about planting the surveillance equipment right under the NVA's nose while we sat around in the hootch, informally debriefing each other on the last days of patrolling. Such bull sessions actually were an invaluable time for us to compare notes. As a group, we had come to know more about the NVA in the Central Highlands than any other unit in the Marine Corps 1st Division, but we learned a lot from each other in those late-night sessions.

Miller's team had run the only patrol outside the Que Sons. He had slipped back into Base Area 112, which was on the other side of the Thu Bon River just east of Laos. His sightings were disturbing. "Dogs," Miller murmured. "The little bastards are using dogs out there to track us. On top of that, now they have small units dressed in our jungle utilities patrolling the area the same way we do. I watched an NVA counterreconnaissance team search for us for two hours yesterday. They're dressing and patrolling like us. I think we have worn out our welcome out there. This is some heavy crap we are beginning to deal with."

Rollings's report only confirmed what Miller had seen in Base Area 112. "I saw guys dressed like us sweep both sides of the trail before the larger movements came out of the dark canyon. Then they would do it again a couple of hours later before a large movement would go into the canyon. These guys are looking for us out there. I didn't see any dogs, but I've got a feeling that's next." Miller and Rollings continued their discussion. It was like iron sharpening iron. The rest of us sat and listened.

Champe finished cleaning his weapon and set it on his cot. Then he pulled his chair into the circle that had formed. Richie put aside his usual aloof attitude and sat down on the floor. He opened a can of beer and handed it to Miller. It felt good being back together again. It wasn't the tent at An Hoa, but the personalities and music were the same. In the background, Joplin was pouring out her guts about Bobby McGee.

That night each of us realized that something bigger than life had taken place in our experiences together with 1st Force. Our aggressive and successful behavior in the bush those past months had not gone unnoticed by the enemy, so the NVA was addressing the problems that 1st Force teams had created. What we wore, how we patrolled, the numbers that we traveled with were being mirrored by the enemy. The window for surviving our style of combat in the Que Sons and Base Area 112 was rapidly closing. Whatever punishment we were to inflict on the NVA would have to be quick and decisive. Change was in the air.

Rollings and I continued to talk after the rest of the lieutenants had called it a night. "Wayne, how about the security element and the cadre? Did you spot them moving in and out of the dark canyon?"

Rollings quickly answered. "Damn right I did, and I think we could take those suckers out if we planned it right. What I think we could do is lay out a claymore mine ambush, with air support on station, and really mop them up. We could set it up at night and spring it when the cadre comes by in the morning. I could set my watch by them for three days. In the morning at 0900 and 1700 in the evening. The jungle is thick enough. I don't think they would spot it."

"I know exactly what you're talking about," I said, "and I think it would work. Ayers and I watched the same morning and evening pattern with that crew a couple of months ago. Throw my team in there, reinforced by, say, Lynn's and Randy's teams as a reaction force circling the area near the objective, and now you have something to back you up. The 5th Marines could saddle up a company-size reaction force and have it ready to go if you need it." Rollings and I got very excited as we war-gamed the plan. Realizing that if the opportunity was wasted the infantry would soon be challenging that huge NVA force on the enemy's terms, Rollings prepared to take the plan to Simmons as quickly as possible.

Once the initial plan was hatched and agreed upon, the

conversation turned to speculation. Having seen the NVA cadre close up, I had to ask Rollings one question. "Do you think it's Front Four?"

Rollings's reply was cautious. "I don't know. Let's just blow them away and let the intelligence guys figure out who they were. I feel the clock ticking on this one, and we don't want to run out of time."

The next morning, a batch of personal mail was delivered to the lieutenants' hootch. At the time, we had been in the field so much that the mail had been piling up. I rummaged through the pile, finding only one letter. It was from my mom. The opening line froze me right in my tracks.

Dear Bill, I find it very difficult to tell you this, but I must. Lee Wallace died in an auto accident last week in South Carolina. He was finishing up his flight training at Cherry Point when he fell asleep at the wheel of his car and struck a tree. That is all we know. The whole town is devastated. I'm sorry I've got to tell you this while you are alone over there. I pray that God will continue to protect you and bring you back safe to us.

The letter dropped from my hands. Numb with grief, I stormed out of the hootch.

Lowder picked up the letter, read it, and handed it to Rollings. One by one, the lieutenants quietly read it for themselves. Finally, Lowder broke the silence. "This guy Wallace was like his brother. Bill told me all about him. They played football in high school and college together. They even joined the Corps together. I think they lived right down the street from each other. This guy was a Marine jet jockey; man, I can't believe he died in a car. What a waste."

Inconsolable, I wandered the perimeter of the compound for the next few hours. The lieutenants left me to walk off my grief. Finally Lowder approached me. "You want to get some chow, bro?"

"No, I'm not hungry. I just can't believe I lost Lee, damn it. Not Lee. Man, he was my brother. I can't believe this."

Lowder's voice softened as he tried to console me. "I don't know what to say, bro. You know we live with this stuff every day. I see you guys board the choppers, and I say to myself, Man, I may never see you or Randy or Ric or Wayne ever again."

"You do that, too? I thought I was the only one with feelings like that. I'd rather be in the bush in the crap myself. It's really hard to listen over a radio back here while you guys are going through it."

"No, I think we all really care about one another."

I hesitated and then broke down. Lowder slipped away to allow me to purge my heart of its grief.

Emotions come and go in war. I knew I would have to put that one behind me and move on or risk losing my edge. That night, I joined a party that I knew the lieutenants were throwing to pull me out of my grief. It worked, and the Paco stories started to surface. The beer and wine flowed until the early-morning hours. Laughter *can* heal a man's soul; somehow the pain of it all lifted, and I could move on. We must have sensed, even more strongly that night, that our life together in 1st Force was about to change. We made a pledge to one another. Miller, who after four years in Vietnam knew better than anyone how fleeting friendships in war can be, opened up the conversation. "You know, we gotta stay in touch when this is all over. I want you guys at my wedding next March in San Francisco. We need to make a pact here or something."

Lowder said, "Yeah, we gotta be there for one another back in the World, no matter what."

Rollings agreed. "I'm there for you guys. Anything I can do for any of you, I'll do it."

Champe, who was usually quiet, offered his commitment without hesitation. "I'll be there for you guys. You can count on it." I said, "Nobody but us will ever believe what we've seen over here; I can't lose track of you guys. Count me in." We lieutenants had become so close in battle that the officers club, the Leaky Teaky, was without our presence most of the time because we liked to hang out together in our hootch.

Simmons liked Rollings's idea for taking out the NVA security element and cadre. He prepared the operation orders. Rollings would act as the tip of the spear in the huge ambush, taking in a reinforced team of eleven men. They would have two M-60 machine guns, twelve claymore mines, and an array of explosives able to cover 150 meters of the road leading into the dark canyon. Reaction forces would be circling in a 46 off in the distance, ready to come to Rollings's assistance if needed. The plan was airtight. Rollings would set up the ambush at night along the road. He would receive assistance from an early-September harvest moon. The cadre had not broken their pattern, approaching along the road in the morning and leaving along it in the afternoon. Rollings had confirmed that just a few days earlier.

Politicians, friend or foe, can become the warrior's worst nightmare. On September 8, 1969, just minutes before 1st Force boarded the choppers to fly into the Que Sons, a cease-fire was announced throughout all of Vietnam in honor of North Vietnam's president, Ho Chi Minh, who had died a few days earlier. The rotor blades on the package of six CH-46 helicopters, four Cobras, and four Huey gunships were already spinning. The teams were headed up toward the helo pad ready to board when word came from III Marine Amphibious Force to cancel the mission. The cease-fire originated at the peace talks in Paris, through the Kissinger team, and received its confirmation through President Richard Nixon. The politicians had succeeded in scrubbing a mission that the 1st Force Marines had prepared, fought, and died over for months.

Rollings sat in the hootch in total disbelief. His freshly camouflaged face could not hide his disgust. I felt that we had been sold out by men who did not have a clue about how to fight a war. Nearly 33,000 of my generation had already died in that hellhole. Now 1st Force had just been robbed of the opportunity of a lifetime to vindicate some of that loss.

The three-day truce spelled the end of the way things had been in the Que Sons. We knew it was over. We knew that there was an abundance of NVA spies at very high levels in the South Vietnamese Army and that our top-secret operations orders by then were probably gracing the walls of Front Four's command bunker.

We were warriors, not politicians. That evening we chased away the political demons with some beer and a new tape by Creedence Clearwater Revival. Randy Champe trashed the Janis Joplin tape, and "Bad Moon Rising" replaced "Bobby McGee."

The cease-fire ended at first light on the fourth day. Early that morning, huge B-52 bombers left the runways of bases in Thailand and flew at high altitudes en route to the Que Son Mountains where their bombs were dropped on the dark canyon. As far away as Hill 34, the impact of the B-52s' bomb run felt like an earthquake. I lay half awake on my cot in our dimly lit hootch. When the earth trembled, I checked my watch and noted that the bombs reached their destination at 0430, right on schedule. The dark canyon had been altered forever. Deep craters marked the jungle floor where dozens of bombs had impacted and whole stands of trees had been blown over by the force of the explosions. But we all concluded that the highly mobile security element and the cadre probably were nowhere near the canyon when the bombs made impact. The massive air strike signaled the beginning of a sweep of the Que Son Mountains and adjoining areas that would net the 5th and 7th Marine regiments some of the largest stashes of NVA weapons and supplies captured during the entire Vietnam War. More Marines were wounded and killed in and around the Que Sons in 1969 than in any of their other tactical areas of responsibility. I am happy to say that the number of NVA casualties far outnumbered our own.

Prior to Marine infantry's operation into the Que Sons, 1st Force was asked to do some reconnaissance work. But as we expected, the NVA was waiting near every possible LZ. Over those few weeks, 1st Force's patrols in the Que Son Mountains and points west turned into one major battle after another. The NVA was committed to wiping us out.

Soon after being inserted into the Que Sons, just a few days after the cease-fire was lifted, Randy Champe made contact with a platoon of NVA that was setting an ambush near his LZ. Moving out ahead of his team, Randy broke the first ambush by himself and recovered documents from the bodies of the dead NVA. He shouted to his team to lay down a base of fire on a second ambush farther up the hill, then broke the second ambush, killing more NVA and capturing their weapons. Finally, totally surrounded, he called for an emergency extract. He tied an air panel onto his back, and in full view of the enemy, he guided the chopper into an LZ, but the helicopter came under heavy

fire and began to bounce as it prepared for liftoff, causing
its rotor blades to vibrate up and down. Randy's radioman,
McLaughlin, was struck in the head and killed instantly.
Still under heavy enemy fire, Champe picked up the radioman and carried him onto the chopper.

A few miles southwest of the Que Sons, Ritchie walked
off his insert chopper and stepped onto a high-speed trail,
then beat an AK-47-packing NVA soldier to the draw in a
point-blank contact. He grabbed the AK-47 from the dead
NVA and was forced back to his LZ by heavy enemy
movement coming down the trail. He called for an emergency extract, and the same chopper that had just inserted
him returned to extract his team.

A few weeks later, Wayne Rollings received the same
kind of greeting that Champe had gotten in the Que Sons.
Ambushes were everywhere Wayne turned. The enemy
fire was so intense that some of his equipment was literally
shot off him in the first ambush. When his point man's
M-16 malfunctioned, he stepped around him, opening up
on the enemy and killing three of them. On the second ambush, Wayne ran out in front of his men to assault the NVA
position, breaking the ambush and killing more of the
enemy. At the third ambush, Rollings totally overpowered
the NVA with small-arms fire and grenades, leaving the
area strewn with dead NVA.

These contacts between the NVA and 1st Force did not
even remotely resemble recon missions; all were conventional firefights between disciplined, well-trained NVA infantry and highly outnumbered Force Recon Marines. The
battles got personal and were being fought to the death.
Most of the time, air support was not even an option; the
NVA and the recon teams were in such close contact that
there was not enough room for napalm or bombs. It was
obvious that the 5th and 7th Marine regiments would

have to engage the enemy; the number of the enemy troops was overwhelming when compared to a Force Recon team.

Ayers and I rolled the dice with the NVA one last time on January 5, 1970. We were inserted into an LZ about fifty meters above a wide river flowing east from the Laotian border. A few months earlier, the NVA had caught a twelve-man army LRRP recon team on the bank of the river, killing eleven American soldiers who were trapped with the river to their backs and the high ground in front of them. Ayers and I knew what had happened to the army Rangers, and we were not going to allow the NVA to push us down to the river (a well-known tactical no-no since at least the fifth century B.C.).

The NVA moved in on us just as soon as our insert chopper had left. I led the men into the jungle and had the team set up a tight perimeter. There the team remained completely quiet and just listened for the enemy. Sure enough, the NVA began to move on line down the mountain toward us. They were spread out far enough that at least one of the enemy soldiers was bound to run into our perimeter.

The temptation to move toward the river was immediate. If Ayers and I had not known the history of the area, we probably would have gone that route. Instead, I requested air support. A Cobra gunship answered my plea and, within a minute, made his first pass over my team's position. The pilot remarked that there were so many NVA that they looked like swarming ants as they moved down the mountain. Telling us to get down, the Cobra came in low level, firing its machine guns and high-explosive rockets into the ranks of the advancing enemy. The NVA unit was caught out in the open and devastated by the Cobra's firepower. The pilot checked with me to make sure he hadn't hit the patrol. Then he ordered me to head for my original insert LZ, where a CH-46 would pick us up. The Cobra pilot assured me that he would cut off the NVA from the extract LZ. With that radio transmission, two more Cobras made low-level passes over us, firing on the still-advancing enemy unit.

I stood up and told Ayers to lead out. I then took tail-end Charlie to make sure all the team made it to the chopper. Even running full speed, the fifty meters to the LZ seemed to take an eternity; all the while, the NVA were firing where they guessed the next step of a Marine might land. But the Cobras hovered above us like guardian angels, firing into the jungle with deadly accuracy.

The extract chopper sat down at the edge of the LZ while enemy bullets tore holes through its thin metal skin and exited the other side. Hanover Sue sprinted the last twenty meters to the chopper. Finally, Ayers and I stood on the tail ramp, firing back into jungle that was lit up with the muzzle flashes from the enemy's weapons. We emptied our magazines into the jungle before fully boarding the chopper. It would probably be the last time we would stand together in combat, and we were milking the opportunity. Finally I hollered, "That's it, Sarge; it's over. Let's get the hell out of here while we can." Heavy weather had moved in, obscuring the mountains with a low cloud cover. The chopper pilot lifted up out of the LZ and headed for the river. He used the river like a winding road to lead him out of the foggy jungle. The clouds closed behind the chopper, covering the river as we flew to safety. A chapter was also closing in my life.

CHAPTER 12

Bittersweet Victory

Paris in the fall can be the loveliest of places. The Majestic Hotel had outlived the destructive forces of numerous wars and had played host to the Nazi officers of the Third Reich thirty years earlier. They, in turn, relinquished its somewhat damaged beauty and comforts to the Allies, who cherished it as a trophy preserved by the French underground. Now, in November of 1969, the Majestic Hotel continued to host what was called the Paris Peace Talks between the U.S. and Hanoi governments over the Vietnam War.

As the U.S. veteran diplomat Henry Cabot Lodge sat in his opulent suite in the old Majestic on a beautiful November morning in 1969, Lodge was neither enjoying this fall season in France nor was he feeling any sense of accomplishment after nearly a year of negotiations. That particular morning, the daily intelligence brief reported that the number of Americans killed in Vietnam had reached 9,202 for the first eleven months of 1969.

Within a few days, Henry Cabot Lodge, first appointed by the Johnson administration as chief U.S. negotiator to the Paris Peace Talks in 1968, had returned to his rural New England home. The beautiful fall colors soon erased the faces of Hanoi's negotiators Xuan Thuy and Mrs. Nguyen Thi Binh from his mind. Lodge tried desperately to purge himself of his failure in Paris. Ambassador Henry Cabot Lodge cleansed himself as much as possible while he walked and talked his way across the New England countryside. He knew he would have to bear his share of the blood guilt for the Vietnam War. No statesmen or politicians of his generation would ever be able to completely free themselves from that responsibility.

President Nixon's acceptance of Lodge's resignation had not gone well. The president cringed at the thought of the North Vietnamese stalling the Paris Peace Talks over the shape of the conference table for the better part of 1969. The day that he received Lodge's formal resignation, the president, filled with anger and emotion, ordered the bombing of North Vietnam to resume.

Nixon's decision not to replace Lodge infuriated Hanoi. Their chief negotiator, Xuan Thuy, boycotted the talks when U.S. career foreign officer and ambassador Philip C. Habib tried to fill the shoes of a special envoy to the talks. The fact was that Habib was not a special envoy. After a year of debating the shape of the conference table, all factions—the United States, Hanoi, Saigon, and the Viet Cong—sat down together at a circular table in the Majestic Hotel. The United States merely ignored the Viet Cong presence at the table while Hanoi ignored Saigon's presence. Second-string negotiators from both the United States and Hanoi continued the stalemate while blood continued to be spilled in the jungles of Vietnam.

In late March 1970, far from the steamy jungles of Vietnam and the beauty of the Majestic Hotel in Paris, another group of men found their places around a circular table. That table was in the beautiful Buena Vista Restaurant at San Francisco's Fisherman's Wharf. The men were a representative group of the 1st Force lieutenants, class of

1969. Lynn Lowder, Jim Ritchie, Ric Miller, and I sipped Irish coffee rather than beer. Wayne Rollings and Randy Champe had just received orders to Hawaii and couldn't make it to San Francisco. On that mid-Saturday morning, more than high-and-tight haircuts distinguished the four of us. We were in our dress blues: it was Ric Miller's wedding day and the morning after his raucous bachelor party.

Six months after their final assault on the Que Son Mountains, the dialogue among the brothers revealed that the homecoming for each of us was bittersweet. We were received by a society indifferent to the service, and sacrifices, of young men of all branches. Not even the mid-morning beverages served by the trendy café could make us feel kindly about America's feelings toward servicemen and the Vietnam War. We were determined, nevertheless, to savor our reunion and to celebrate that special day with our wild, wacky, soon-to-married buddy. We recognized that Miller was the least prepared of all of us to make a lifetime commitment just then, but we were all present to celebrate and commiserate with the unwitting bride.

In the midst of the busy café, with the sound of the Pacific Ocean's waves crashing against the rocks in the background, we were in a world of our own. We had traded the tent at An Hoa and the tin-roofed hootch on Hill 34 for our present setting. The brotherhood reminisced about the wild, often fearful, year we spent together humping the mountainous jungles of Vietnam.

Miller, who was as loony as ever but considerably less crazy than he'd been his last six months in Nam, announced that he was still gonna party even though the wedding was less than three hours away. He said, "I needed to fortify myself. My woman's parents are a little stiff. You'll see." I consented to find a better bar with him, then Miller challenged the other three to do a recon with him to find another pit stop. Lowder and Ritchie tried to persuade Miller that with the wedding just a few hours away, the timing was not right for the recon, but Miller was unmoved by their logic. He stood up unsteadily and a .25-caliber revolver tumbled from under his blue tunic. Unembarrassed, Miller explained—he was going into marriage armed as heavily as he was in Vietnam. He added, laughing, "Besides, you never know when you're gonna run into an obnoxious hippie; they're all over this damn city." Miller and I sauntered out of the bar, looking for trouble.

Three hours later, two hundred relatives and friends were perched on, and around, the steps of the chapel on Treasure Island on San Francisco Bay. Lowder and Ritchie were off to one flank, shaking their heads and acknowledging Miller's consistent lunacy. The bride's father, who managed to convey a haughty demeanor, was real agitated. The bride was seen trying to assuage him. Ten minutes later, the bride's new, yellow VW, piloted by Miller with me riding shotgun, rounded a corner and approached the church. The hood of the car was dented, and the body looked off-center. At the front of the church, Miller leaped out, smiling, and gathered himself. No one was pleased, but all were relieved, and the wedding proceeded.

The festivities lasted until late afternoon. The wrecked VW sat in front of the San Francisco Marine Memorial Club. A sign in white shoe polish read JUST MARRIED on the back window. Inside, Ric and his bride waved their good-byes to friends and family. We stood at attention with champagne glasses raised for one last toast to our brother and each other. When Ric pulled away from the club, a link in the chain that had bound us so closely together was broken. Within minutes, I was bidding my fellow lieutenants farewell.

I had come full circle. I felt drawn back to San Francisco State. As I headed west over the Bay Bridge, I felt my visit to the campus was a pilgrimage that had to be made. My relationship with Pam had ended very unceremoniously that morning with one phone call. I searched for meaning in what was then a five-year journey. From the mid-sixties until that very day in 1970, I felt as though I had experienced a war on three fronts. The first front was on the campus of San Francisco State. It was a battleground mostly of ideas, fought from the classroom to the Commons and from one end of the campus to the other. The emotional causes, some which strongly moved me, were legion: racial equality, social justice in all its dimensions, alleged Establishment oppression and authoritarianism, sexual freedom, and a whole range of traditional values that was continuously under fire.

I smiled when the headlights of my car swept across the campus as I sped through a familiar alley between the football stadium and the physical education building. I continued smiling, remembering some of the ludicrous antics perpetuated largely by the extremists of all persuasions on campus in the late sixties. Oh yes, I thought, my generation took itself very seriously in those heady college years when we were coming of age. But it was a terrifying time, also, when the radical students of my generation, their faculty collaborators, and their cohorts off campus across the land, moved by the social and political passions of the day, sought to crush anyone who opposed their ideas or stood for what they considered the unredeeming status quo. To this day, I am appalled at how the institutions of this nation had been shaken to their very foundations.

I stopped my car on a knoll at one end of the campus. I

left the headlights on, which illuminated the center of the campus where the first front of the war continued to be played out daily. I stepped from the car with my medals glittering in the pitch-black night as rays of light picked up their brilliance. I stood on the high ground looking over the battlefield that I had fought on and conquered. I knew the truth about the Vietnam War that my antagonists would never know. I had paid the price and earned the right to enjoy the most important fruit of the victory that was only to be heard.

Vietnam was, of course, the second front—and the real war—and the event that galvanized, then split, the nation and seemed to embody as subsets many of the other social and political causes of the sixties. The Vietnam War inspired the political and social passions of people across this land. The war also changed everyone who went and fought. I had lost my father, Lee Wallace, and Gene Ayers during my time in service to my country. Yes, Ayers ran a patrol a few weeks after I left and was missing in action. Nevertheless, I still felt the victory. The war had also given something back to me: it had given me meaningful relationships formed in the crucible of combat. My contemporaries of all ranks who went off to war enjoyed a sacred comradeship, forged in battle. While in Vietnam, we rarely spoke much about that bond, or gave much thought to it, but the recognition of that silent mutual commitment to one another's welfare was always there. I had come to realize that experiencing war with other men who, like me, had chosen to serve, created ties that would endure forever, even if never renewed. And that, of course, was the nature of the brother love I had shared, and would continue to share, with the memory of Sgt. Gene Ayers.

I had, indeed, conquered the first two battlefronts of the war. I stood proud, mature, honorable, like a champion overlooking the San Francisco State campus. The revelation I had that very night, while savoring the victory, was that there was a third front of the war that I must soon face without my uniform and without my warrior brothers. The third front for myself and the other veterans of the Vietnam War would be our return to an indifferent and even disdainful nation. A nation whose leaders had not only sent us off to risk our lives in Vietnam but had set us up for failure by denying us, through political and military policy, the means to win on the battlefield. One thing I knew I could count on once I got home was the common bonds and trust I shared with my 1st Force brothers.

But even beyond that, my own father's words spoken two years earlier, "Don't forget God," had not left my mind or spirit. The chaplain's words to me at Quantico, "Go to Vietnam. God has something for you there," had proved true. The life-changing words of my father and the chaplain, coupled with Sergeant Mormon's godly influence during our pathfinder mission, eventually became pivotal in my decision to spend the rest of my life serving the Lord my God.

Epilogue

In the spring of 1970, just two months after returning from Vietnam, I received a letter bearing the return address of the 1st Force Recon Company commander. The new company commander informed me that Sgt. Eugene Ayers had been lost on a patrol that had taken place on March 19. At the time, I was serving as the officer in charge of the noncommissioned officer leadership school at Marine Corps Base Twentynine Palms, California. I was sitting alone in my office when I received the letter. I sat speechless for several minutes, remembering that just a few weeks before I had spent most of my last day in Vietnam with Sergeant Ayers. He had stuck to me like glue that day, reserved a jeep, and personally drove me to the port at Da Nang where I boarded a ship for the States. A troop withdrawal had cut a month from my tour, and very suddenly I was out of the bush and headed home. Sergeant Ayers refused to just drop me off, staying with me for the several hours that passed before I was allowed to board. It was as if he was having a hard time saying good-bye; at the time I just figured he was being what we all loved about him, "Mother." I now know how precious that last day with him really was. I have chosen not to write about his fatal patrol, although I have researched it thoroughly over the years. In 1972, my wife, Barbara, and I hosted

Sergeant Ayers's mother, Vera Ayers, for a week's visit at our home. Doc Perry, who was the corpsman on the patrol that cost Sergeant Ayers his life, met with Mrs. Ayers and myself. He gave us a detailed accounting of what really happened on the patrol and why Sergeant Ayers's body was not recovered. Although Sergeant Ayers and I ran twenty Force Recon patrols together, I have had to condense his character and valor into the few patrols I have shared in this book. As a result of his last patrol, he was listed as missing in action and became the posthumous recipient of the nation's second-highest combat award, the Navy Cross, for heroic actions on March 19, 1970, which saved the lives of the young members of his recon team. He would say that he was just doing his job, but I think the Gospel of Saint John, chapter 15, verse 13, probably says it best: "Greater love hath no man than this, that a man lay down his life for his friends."

I know that, in 1969, First Force Recon Company beat the North Vietnamese Army at its own game in the Central Highlands of South Vietnam. From March through November, the company's patrols sighted 7,747 enemy soldiers. Three Marines, Sgt. Gene Ayers, Sgt. Joe Crockette, and Lt. Wayne Rollings, were awarded the Navy Cross for gallantry in action. The other personal decorations that were awarded individually to the men of First Force were two Legion of Merits, eleven Silver Stars, thirty-two Bronze Stars, twenty-one Navy Commendation Medals, twenty-two Navy Achievement Medals, and forty-three Purple Hearts. All save the Purple Hearts were awarded for individual valor above and beyond the call of duty.

A letter of recommendation, dated March 10, 1970, for 1st Force Recon Company's Meritorious Unit Citation summed up the unit's value and valor:

Specific missions of the company ranged from the penetration of deep and long range reconnaissance patrols into the very heart of enemy controlled territory to locate enemy troop concentrations, and to the capture of enemy personnel. In the face of numerically superior enemy forces who were employing aggressive, well trained counter-reconnaissance forces, the company repeatedly reentered enemy sanctuaries, completing assigned missions and providing information vital to the subsequent fixing, interdiction and destruction of untold numbers of enemy forces. Accomplishing a total of 191 patrols, the information gathered by patrols formed the foundation and impetus for operations and massive air/artillery strikes against enemy base camps, lines of communications and supply depots. The identity and location of the newly infiltrated 90th NVA Regiment into Quang Nam Province, the egress of the 21st and 1st NVA Regiments from Quang Nam Province and subsequent return of these units was established in large measure by information gathered by the company's patrols. Intelligence gathered from information provided by these patrols went on to precipitate highly successful forays, including Operation Durham Peak, by the 1st Marine Division into the Que Son Mountains and Antenna Valley area where extremely complex enemy base camps and large quantities of supplies were uncovered and destroyed. The enemy was denied a vital stepping stone to Da Nang from the south and to An Hoa from the east and his designs for offensive operations against these areas were effectively pre-empted. While embarked on operations for the III Marine Amphibious Force, the company was tasked to locate the enemy's Military Region 5 and Front Four Headquarters, their related installations and supply and communications routes in the south-western reaches of Quang Nam Province. Patrols provided a flow of heretofore unknown and extremely valuable information from the interior of the enemy's base areas. With repeated interdiction of his newly identified installations, and facilities, the enemy was effectively kept off balance and rendered unable to launch a "1969 summer offensive" of the magnitude he had intended.

Over the past thirty years I have watched the lieutenants and officers of 1st Force Recon Company, class of 1969, also succeed in their personal lives. Wayne Rollings has risen to the rank of major general in the Marine Corps. Lynn Lowder became an attorney, started his own law firm, and currently serves as general counsel for a Fortune 500 company. Ric Miller is a much-sought-after captain of industry and currently serves as CEO for a major international corporation. Jim Ritchie became a successful dentist. Randy Champe was Crewman of the Year for the Los Angeles Police Department's Air Support Unit in 1990. He was awarded the Policeman's Medal of Valor for unselfishly diverting his disabled police helicopter from a busy school playground on June 13, 1991, an action that cost him his life. Bob Hansen retired as a colonel and started his own marketing firm. Roger Simmons retired as a colonel and went into commercial landscaping. Dal Williams retired as a major and became successful in city government.

In May 1971, two weeks before I left the Marine Corps, realizing that I had not successfully completed my tour in Vietnam on my own, I surrendered my life to the Lord Jesus Christ, went on to complete my education, and was ordained into the ministry. Currently my work, Angel Fire Ministries, serves this nation with a special emphasis on

Vietnam veterans, helping them deal with the ever-present friction that inhibits success in their lives. My call and destiny is this:

> And they shall beat their swords into plow-
> shares, and their spears into pruning hooks;
> nation shall not lift up sword against nation,
> neither shall they learn war any more.
> Isaiah 2:4b

FORCE RECON DIARY, 1969
by Bruce H. Norton

FORCE RECON DIARY, 1969 is the riveting, true-to-life account of survival, heroism, and death in the elite Marine 3d Force Recon unit, one of only two Marine units to receive the Valorous Unit Citation during the Vietnam War. Doc Norton, a former 3d Force Recon medic and retired Marine major, recounts his unit's experiences behind enemy lines during the tense patrols, sudden ambushes, and acts of supreme sacrifice that occurred as they gathered valuable information about NVA operations right from the source.

FORCE RECON DIARY, 1970
by Bruce H. Norton

Operating beyond the artillery fan of friendly forces, in the thick of a jungle war, the Marines of 1st and 3d Force Recon companies understood that the only things keeping them alive in "Indian Country" were their own skills and courage and the loyalty they had to one another. Here is the continuing saga of life behind enemy lines by a former member of these fearless and peerless Force Recon companies.

Published by Ivy Books.
Available in bookstores everywhere.

FORCE RECON COMMAND
3rd Force Recon Company in Vietnam, 1969–70

by Lt. Col. Alex Lee, USMC (Ret.)

In order to prevent surprise attacks on U.S. forces as they were pulling out of Vietnam in 1969, someone had to be able to pinpoint the NVA's movements. That dangerous job was the assignment of then-major Alex Lee and the Marines of the 3rd Force Reconnaissance Company. Whether tracking NVA movements, recovering downed air crews, or making bomb-damage assessments after B-52 strikes, each time one of Lee's small, well-led, and wildly outnumbered teams was airlifted into the field, the men never knew if the day would end violently.

Forthright and unabashed, Lieutenant Colonel Lee leaves no controversy untouched and no awe-inspiring tale untold in this gripping account.

Published by Ivy Books.
Available in bookstores everywhere.